the Healthy Home Workbook

the Healthy Home Workbook

Easy Steps for Eco-Friendly Living

by Kimberly Rider

Photographs by Thayer Allyson Gowdy

CHRONICLE BOOKS

SAN FRANCISCO

Library of Congress Cataloging-in-Publication Data:
Rider, Kimberly.
The healthy home workbook: easy steps for eco-friendly living /
Kimberly Rider ; photographs by Thayer Allyson Gowdy.
p. cm.
Includes bibliographical references and index.
ISBN 0-8118-5077-3
1. Home economics. 2. Dwelling-Environmental aspects. I. Title.
TX303.R75 2006
640–dc22   2005016126

Manufactured in China.
Design by Celery Design Collaborative
Styling by Leigh Noë

Distributed in Canada by Raincoast Books
9050 Shaughnessy Street
Vancouver, British Columbia V6P 6E5

10 9 8 7 6 5 4 3 2 1

Chronicle Books LLC
85 Second Street
San Francisco, California 94105

www.chroniclebooks.com

This book was manufactured using
environmentally responsible materials
from sustainable sources.

This book is dedicated to those who pursue a thoughtful life. A joyful spirit can bring meaning to any aspect of your home and lifestyle.

Contents

Introduction

Your home is your haven, your retreat, your sanctuary from the outside world. Most of us spend over a third of our lives at home and care deeply about the quality of our home environment. It's our place to relax, rejuvenate, feed, nurture and shelter our families and ourselves.

The textures, colors, and experiences of our homes are often multilayered in both physical and spiritual aspects. To strive for a home that offers sanctuary and enrichment is noble and natural. Every choice you make when you create your home environment is important in that it is an opportunity to select materials and practices that can improve your family's and your own health. In the long view, a healthy household is healthier for the environment as well.

Our nesting instincts create a powerful desire to make our homes as attractive and healthy as possible. But what if you don't understand which factors actually create a sound living environment? What if you can't identify which materials, objects, and ingredients could be detrimental to your health? Pinpointing hazards, even for the vigilant, can be difficult at best.

The Healthy Home Workbook will open your doors to the world of a natural, nontoxic lifestyle. The focus of this book is on simple shifts that create dramatic results. From bathing to sleeping to cooking, every choice you make has an impact on the environment that you create at home.

The beauty of the overall philosophy of a Healthy Home is that it makes our everyday tasks and rituals special and meaningful. Our modern world tends to keep us focused on work, driving, shopping, and coping with lots of activity. This book will remind you to pay attention to the things that matter and give you choices about the products you decide to keep in your house as well as the habits you have. Reading this book will be an invitation to have things in your home that you love, and it will give you good reasons to make changes in your purchasing decisions that could dramatically improve your health and the enjoyment of your home environment. You will be offered simple steps you can take to improve your house's air quality, materials, as well as household practices. Based on your commitment level, you can make changes so that the transition to a Healthy Home is gradual and continually inspiring. Resources and fun projects will give you hands-on contact with the multitude of Healthy Home alternatives.

Buildings of the past were made with wood, brick, stone, glass, plaster, and cement. Furniture was made of solid wood, oiled to keep it polished. Rugs or carpets were made of wool or cotton. Insulation was built in by making walls thick, and roofing was constructed from wood shingles or tiles of clay or stone. Walls were plastered. Windows were made to be opened, so at least in good weather there was plenty of natural ventilation. But toxic materials also were present in homes of the past. Not knowing enough about their hazards, housewives used such chemicals as arsenic, lead, and mercury to perform certain household chores. Interior and exterior paints were often made with lead; many people are still living with the legacy of childhood lead poisoning caused by eating chips of paint. Asbestos, called a miracle mineral when its fire-resistant properties were discovered, is now known to be a cancer causer that contaminates hundreds of thousands of residences, schools, and other buildings in this country.

We do not need to return to the ways of the past to avoid exposure to house toxics, but we can take some lessons from the past for a better future. This can be as simple as fresh air and natural materials.

As modern home construction methods have improved energy efficiency, our houses have become more sealed and enclosed. The introduction of synthetic materials and household chemicals into this contained space can contribute to poor air quality. The lack of continual air exchange can exacerbate this poor air quality, causing your home to undermine your health rather than nurture it. Recently, tests of indoor air quality have resulted in evidence that our indoor quality can be as much as ten times as polluted as the outdoor air.

In the last thirty years, there has been a dramatic increase in childhood asthma and other respiratory ailments. If you or anyone you know suffers from allergies, chronic fatigue, or unexplained symptoms, this could be sick building syndrome or multiple chemical sensitivity. This book is not intended to diagnose or treat unknown or severe illnesses, but you may find that after reading *The Healthy Home Workbook,* you'll want to explore the subject further or see how it might relate to other spaces where you spend time.

But here's the good news. Even if you're a busy person, as most of us are, some very simple steps will make your house healthier. You don't have to overhaul your home—though you may find yourself doing that over time. By making just a few changes in lifestyle and purchasing decisions, you can make improvements in the health of your home, and armed with a bit of knowledge, these can add up to giant steps towards health.

As you flip through the pages of *The Healthy Home Workbook,* you'll find out how to remove the most commonly found dangerous or toxic materials from your home and to create a nurturing and beneficial environment for you and your family.

You will find more peace of mind knowing that your home is healthy for your family. You can improve the enjoyment of your home with higher quality materials, lower maintenance requirements and costs, and make it more durable, and quieter. Have you tried, and failed, to get straight answers to simple questions about materials, chemicals, or ingredients in products? This book can help you understand the most basic principles about toxin-free living. You have the power to choose any level of commitment that you want.

Educating yourself about the basic principles of a Healthy Home will enable you to make decisions that allow you to relax in the knowledge that you've made your house a true haven. You'll gain information that will let you exert greater control over your environment and your potential for a healthier lifestyle.

This easy-to-follow book lets you assess the health of your home room by room, beginning with your entryway and ending in the garden. Each chapter focuses on the most problematic issues of health affecting different areas of the house. Once you determine the trouble spots, you get to choose from three levels of remedy based on cost, time commitment, and intensity of the problem.

You'll find helpful lists that outline issues you will face, such as common household chemicals, product ingredients, and alternatives. These provide you with a quick reference list to take shopping or to help you check labels as you reject or relocate certain items. Simple suggestions and projects offer ways for you and your family to actively learn about the common practices that enhance or hinder the creation of a healthy home environment. The comprehensive resource guide gives you motivation to jumpstart your projects.

One of the wonderful transitions that you will experience in reading this book is a return to a simpler way of life. Simple design that makes use of high-quality components is often better than too many items of lesser quality. It seems obvious that, just like an exquisitely prepared meal, the ingredients that you choose make all the difference. The same is true for your Healthy Home—all of the materials, objects, and products that fill your house contribute to the environment you live in. If you start with the idea of keeping it simple, using high-quality, nontoxic ingredients, you have a recipe for success! It shouldn't cost more, and in some cases you will even save money turning your house into a Healthy Home.

The Healthy Home Workbook will empower you, inspire you, and give you the motivation to make a dramatic change in your home life. Do just a few things in this book and you will see how easy it is to transform your lifestyle. Do a little more and you'll be amazed at the world of healthy living that is at your fingertips! Here's to you, your health, and your new Healthy Home!

A Healthy Home...

- Is inviting and welcoming

- Is bright and warm, with as much natural light as possible

- Is inspired by and connected to the rhythms of nature

- Is simple, clean, and relaxing

- Is respectful of the earth and uses resources wisely

- Has layers of natural materials, rich textures, inspiring colors

- Is comfortable, practical, functional, and efficient

- Utilizes nontoxic, high-quality materials and objects

- Is unique: the style and objects have meaning for those who live there

- Encourages physical, mental, and spiritual health

- Evolves and changes with the needs of the household

CHAPTER 1

Living Areas & Entryways

Living rooms and family rooms are places in the home where friends and family gather, pets lounge, and multiple activities occur.

These areas are especially important because they tend to occupy the largest overall square footage, making the materials and objects here high contributors to your home's health, especially air quality. A healthy living environment is light-filled, accessible to fresh air, and furnished to function well and look attractive. With a welcoming and meaningful aesthetic for those who use the room, larger living spaces shared by family members and guests can have a mix of objects and stylistic themes. An important factor to consider is what these rooms and their contents are made of. You will accomplish much of what can create a healthy home if furniture, construction, and decoration materials are natural and nontoxic.

The Entry *A Shoeless House*

In many cultures people remove their shoes when they come home or visit others. The transition from outdoors to indoors has practical implications as well as the symbolic one of treating home as a sacred space. Removing shoes to come indoors is a way to avoid tracking outdoor pollutants, pesticides, germs, and chemicals into our homes. As this simple step can be the first way we reduce pollutants in the home environment, it makes sense to pay attention to the more subtle emotional aspect of this practice. You might find it is a good way to change the pace of your day and recognize that you are stepping into a different aspect of your life: your home life.

You might find yourself inspired to embellish the ritual and the entry of your home to signify that you have arrived at an important moment in your day. Set up a special place to sit near your front door. This can create a soothing way to welcome yourself home by experiencing the ancient ritual of removing your shoes at the threshold, taking a moment to relax and unwind and think about how you want to feel when you are at home. This is a place of intention.

You can suggest to your guests that you have a "shoeless" house by having a clear place to store shoes and personal belongings. You may find that some friends and guests quickly become aware of your preference; you can choose to make a friendly sign to encourage people to remove their shoes. Be flexible—it would be great if everyone adopted your stance, but this may take time or you may have to make exceptions to make your guests feel comfortable.

The front hall closet should accommodate hooks for backpacks and purses, dog leashes, and umbrellas, and hangers for coats. A decorative bowl or covered box to hold keys and wallets near the entry makes these items accessible, but a drawer may be better for safekeeping and keeps clutter at bay. An area rug over a tile or wood floor can easily be picked up and cleaned.

Instant Gratification

Make a floral statement about the vision for your home

Natural materials and seasonal blooms are a way to pay homage to nature's bounty. But commercial flowers are usually grown with dangerous pesticides and chemically fertilized. The best source for an entry table bouquet is your own organic garden, or try to buy organically grown flowers.

Better yet, buy an organically grown blooming plant such as an orchid. Freshly pruned, leafy or bare branches make an interesting architectural element, a display that is art in itself. Don't use bleach or flower food with cut flowers, just put one drop of natural dishwashing liquid in the water or a squeeze of lemon to keep the water fresh. A soap-based insect spray on plants' soil will deter gnats and other insects.

More Committed?

Create a special storage space

Build a modular storage space from wooden or woven cubes for shoes and backpacks, covered to keep dirt and dust to a minimum.

A Truly Healthy Home

A mudroom

Decorate the entryway to be welcoming and serene, symbolic of the feeling you want to create for your entire home. Besides a place for flowers and style, consider creating a mudroom if you have the space, or if you enter your home through a back or side entrance. It can have closed storage and flooring that can be easily mopped when wet and muddy. This should be an organized space where things have their place, but this too can make room for stripping off the day's stresses in ways more than symbolic!

Flooring & Carpets

You have many alternatives if you choose to install or replace flooring in your home, and you can consider temporary fixes as well as more long-term solutions. Problems with traditional flooring include toxics in synthetic materials and the fumes of chemical finishes for hard surfaces like wood and tile. Vinyl flooring off-gasses unhealthy chemicals; synthetic linoleum isn't much better. Synthetic carpet fibers are made from petrochemicals, tufted to backing materials of highly reactive compounds, colored with chemical dyes, and further treated to be antistatic, antimicrobial, and stain-resistant. The adhesives used in carpet glue are especially noxious. Carpet pads are typically made of prime urethane, foamed with hydrocarbons such as methyl butane or bonded urethane, offering their own petrochemical hazards. Carpet also poses the problem of increasing dust and dirt collection and is a perfect environment for mold and fungus to grow, even with very little moisture present.

Evaluate the Health of Your Carpets

If you have a synthetic carpet with urethane backing, even regular vacuuming and steam-cleaning won't eliminate toxins, viruses, bacteria, animal dander, or dust mites. And any carpet that has been damp for twenty-four hours is certain to harbor mold. If you have young children who often play on the floor, you'll want to think about healthy alternatives.

You might consider installing hard flooring or replacing your carpet with a green-certified carpet and natural pad. While it won't eliminate all the problems, it will make a big difference in keeping you and your family healthy. You might also want to think about natural-fiber area rugs that can be easily removed for washing. Although many people prefer wall-to-wall carpeting for its warmth, insulating your floors (with nontoxic insulation) might prove a healthier and better investment in the long run.

Healthy Cleaning for Carpets

Several companies sell nontoxic carpet shampoo that may help lift some of the chemicals out of the materials. This is only a way to decrease the chemical off-gassing of carpets and not the best solution. It can provide some improvement of air quality because the final layer of finishing chemicals, stain protection, and fire retardants can be lifted from the carpet surface. Be sure to clean your carpet during dry weather, open all windows, and if necessary, turn up your heat to ensure that the carpets dry quickly to prevent mold and mildew. You can also sprinkle baking powder on carpets to absorb moisture and odors before vacuuming. (See the cleaning section at the back of the book.)

Hard Floors

Depending on the use the area gets, you can consider different methods and different looks for most hard floor surfaces. If you have an old rustic wood floor and like a rustic whitewashed look, you can sand and paint your floors (be sure you close off other areas of the house first and use a dust collection system while sanding). Once the floors are sanded to a raw state, you can paint on a white or pale water-based, nontoxic paint. Let it dry and then sand again to expose parts of the wood. This look is especially nice in a beach house where bleached driftwood might be gathered on daily walks and find its way into your decor.

You can paint stencils and patterns for an eclectic look or stain and clear-coat hardwood. Nontoxic, water-based dark ebony, glossy white, or even metallic paint can create the palette for a modern look. If you have an older vinyl or synthetic linoleum floor, you can paint it as well. Paint can be highly toxic, especially the high-traffic deck paints, so be sure you research paint lowest in volatile organic compounds (VOCs) for your purpose, and don't be afraid to experiment on a small area first to test its application method and durability.

Research woods such as maple, fir, oak, or cherry that are certified by the Forest Stewardship Council as truly sustainably harvested. The most eco-friendly choice is remilled salvaged woods from demolitions, available from specialist suppliers or your own scouting. This recycling is an ethical way to use old-growth lumber such as redwood and many exotic woods for your remodeling and building projects. Look at every step of the process to understand whether this product is healthy—it's the installation and finishing that make can make a difference. Ask questions of your suppliers and contractor and insist on a nontoxic finish and proper dust collection and cleanup during installation.

Bamboo now comes in a wide variety of colors, finishes, sizes, and styles for flooring. Bamboo is exceptionally hard and grows rapidly, so its harvest is less damaging to the environment than that of mature or old-growth wood. Again, the manufacturing, processing, and installation will determine how healthy the product is for your home, so consider hiring an installer who specializes in healthy homes and understands the air-quality issues that come from wood products. You can find wood preservatives, waxes, linseed oil finishes, and water-based shellacs that are nontoxic and off-gas fairly quickly. Plan to spend time away from the house during installation, and be sure you air it out until the floor is completely cured.

Other alternatives

- Install an unconventional floor such as cork or natural linoleum.
- Stone, porcelain, and ceramic tiles are great for bathrooms and entries.

Generally, these hard flooring materials are healthy but the grout, sealants, and thin-set mixtures used to set and install them are not. Make sure you select installation materials that are nontoxic.

Instant Gratification

Throw rugs

If you have carpeting that is there to stay, especially newer carpet, throw down a lovely natural-fiber area rug over it to limit the amount of chemicals that are released into the air.

More Committed?

Alternatives

If carpet is your flooring choice, take a look at the healthy alternatives to standard carpet. Consider organic wool, hemp, sisal, jute, or coir for your carpeted areas. Even corn is now being synthesized into fiber for carpet! A mix of hard floors covered in area rugs and softer areas that are carpeted with natural materials can create balance and diversity in your home. Be sure any new carpet, including synthetics, is Green Label Plus Certified Carpet.

Select a natural fiber or felt pad and get the thickest pad you can afford for greater comfort. Consider carpet tile so that you can replace sections of carpet instead of an entire area as carpet wears. If appropriate for your application, consider installing a vapor barrier first to limit the exposure of the carpet pad and backing to floors below.

Is there wood under that old carpet?

In a few hours you can pull up old carpet and pad (be sure to wear a dust mask). Paint or coat damaged or raw floors with a nontoxic product.

A Truly Healthy Home

Warm, eco-friendly wood floors

A great way to "recycle" is to sand, stain, and refinish wood floors with nontoxic stains and sealant. If you don't have wood already, install a salvaged wood or certified sustainably harvested wood floor. You can also install a green certified prefinished wood floor (which can be installed over a concrete floor because it is a floating installation).

Furniture & Fabric

Furniture should provide places to gather comfortably. Functional furniture of high quality will provide surfaces that are easy to clean and natural fabrics that hold up well to lots of use. If you pick the highest quality furniture you can afford in neutral, soothing colors for large furniture items, your furniture will last generations. To create a distinct style that is able to shift with the seasons and your mood, you can add color to living spaces with paint, textiles, decorative pillows, and objects of meaning, including art and collections.

The biggest problem anyone will face when considering furniture is the furniture industry itself. Fabric is synthetically made and chemically treated for stain resistance and fire safety. The compounds used have been found to cause severe reactions in some individuals and have been linked to hormone disruption. Cushioning is made from petrochemical products, and metal can exacerbate electromagnetic fields. Furniture is often made of what looks like wood but is actually a type of fiberboard, bound by noxious glues and treated with formaldehyde. True wood furniture is usually mass-produced in ways that maximize profit and is likely made from wood that is not sustainably harvested. It takes some sleuthing to find a healthy alternative.

The materials you use to decorate your home should engage you. Spend some time considering the different feel, look, and smell of natural materials. Aged and supple leather, hand-softened linen, cool rustic stone, durable wool, and luxurious mohair are all examples of fabrics that, when produced without pesticides and processed minimally, can be inspiring textures for your home environment. They naturally resist mold and bugs and, when chosen for the amount of wear and tear you expect, can be excellent choices for your healthy home.

Read the product labels to survey your furniture and find out what it is made of. You should also let your nose and your hands guide you while you study your responses to your current furniture and while you are out shopping: touching and "sniffing" any products that you find attractive. Stiff, slippery, or coated-feeling furniture is either synthetic or coated with fabric treatments. Pay attention to the smells and reactions you have while sitting on your furniture and while you shop: your initial sensitivity to chemicals, dyes, and finishes is telling you something!

PROJECT

A Healthy Pillow

You will need:
- Sewing machine
- Cotton or wool fill
- Unbleached or non-toxic dyed fabric and thread to match

This project can be especially fun if you look beyond new fabrics (although it is rewarding to learn about the variety of companies now offering organic, nontreated and nonsynthetically dyed textiles). Think about other sources of fabric that you have around the house such as old linen tea towels, lace that isn't being used, old wool sweaters or garments that no longer fit or were shrunk in the dryer by accident. These fabrics can be mixed and matched to sew pillows that have two different sides (to change with the seasons), contrasting borders, interesting trim, and patchwork effects. Don't be afraid to use natural objects, buttons, or beads to embellish your pillows. This might inspire a bedroom accent pillow or living room floor cushion. Some people are even brave enough to tackle reupholstering a small chair.

Instant Gratification

Soft comfort

Begin replacing synthetic soft goods (pillows, curtains, rugs) with natural materials and fabrics such as organically grown cotton, linen, and hemp (available through mail order).

More Committed?

Green furniture

Replace fiberboard and plywood furniture with sustainably harvested wood and non-formaldehyde particleboard. Plywood, medium density fiberboard, particleboard, and other wood composites that make up most newer furniture are full of chemicals, including formaldehyde. Several companies do not use these treated wood products and opt for nontoxic versions of the same material. Some European countries have enacted strict environmental standards for consumer products; the United States is less stringent, so consider looking for healthy imports. Ask local retailers or manufacturers that you buy from questions about toxic materials. The process of replacing furniture can be costly and takes time; in the meanwhile, you can recoat especially worrisome furniture with nontoxic wood finish to limit the amount of chemicals released from the wood.

Some of us are lucky to inherit wood furniture that is produced the old-fashioned way. Rediscover an old beauty and repair, refinish, or paint your favorite antique with zero-VOC paint or nontoxic stain and finish. Using antiques and older furniture can be a solution (especially if in good repair or refinished with a nontoxic sealant) because many of the volatile compounds will have out-gassed already over the lifetime of the object. Shellac (derived from insects) is also an option as it is a natural product with nontoxic fumes (it smells strong because of the alcohol content).

Have your upholstered items recovered and filled with new padding made from wool, organic cotton, or natural latex (as long as you are not allergic to latex). You can do this yourself, but it is an undertaking. If you have a professional do the work, be sure they understand your concerns about nontoxic materials and order your fabric from a reputable source that specializes in healthy homes or who can provide an organic certification. Often the cost of reupholstering a sofa will equal the cost of a new one, so look into buying a new, healthy piece of furniture and compare the cost and longevity of the item to redoing an old piece. If you are in love with that comfy armchair, it may be worth it!

A Truly Healthy Home

Purchase new furniture from nontoxic resources

Use these guidelines for fabrics and frames: check for low-impact dyes, no fire retardants or stain treatments in the fabrics, natural filling and support systems such as wool, cotton, or non-polyurethane foam made from latex, and wood with no preservatives or toxic glues.

Custom-made healthy furniture

Have furniture custom made from non-polyurethane foam and natural material so you know exactly how it was made. You may want to consider hiring an interior designer who knows about custom-made healthy furniture or work with a manufacturer that will let you specify materials.

Paint, Wallpaper & Finishes

Paint is one of the largest contributors to poor air quality. Old houses commonly have residues of toxic lead-based paint that you can be exposed to when paint is removed by sanding, scraping, or burning. Lead paint in older houses is a serious health hazard, especially to children. All petroleum-based paints (including latex) are a major source of volatile organic compounds, some of which are carcinogens or cause liver or kidney damage. In small doses they can cause dizziness, disorientation, headaches, loss of muscle control, and irregular heartbeat. Thousands of synthetic chemicals are used in the manufacturing process such as pigments, binders, stabilizers, insecticides, fungicides, solvents, and preservatives. While mercury can no longer be used as a preservative in interior latex paints, it is still allowed in exterior paints. Other heavy metals such as cadmium are still permitted in interior formulas.

Many companies now produce wall finish products that are zero-VOC or lower VOC paints that still may be toxic due to chemicals added to remove odors. There are, however, other paint and wall finishes (including revived ancient techniques), products made from tree and plant oils and resins, herbal extracts, mineral and vegetable pigments, citrus-peel thinners, and beeswax. Milk and casein paint, plaster, and natural grass and fabric wall coverings now produced with nontoxic dyes and adhesives are also healthy choices.

If you intend to paint indoors, no matter how safe the paint, take a few precautions. The best time to paint is in the hot, dry months when you can provide 100 percent ventilation by opening windows. Heat also speeds up the drying process. Anyone who already has health problems should leave the building until the fumes are no longer detectable.

Conventional paints

Readily available at hardware stores; uniform look and coverage. Made with water-based or oil-based solvents and petrochemically derived pigments that tend to off-gas, creating toxins and environmental pollution during production and disposal; contain fungicides, mold inhibitors. Health hazard varies depending on level of VOCs: low-VOC and zero-VOC paints exist, but they are not 100 percent harmless.

Ancient wall colors

Usually made locally with pigment from natural materials, mixed on-site with available resources. Variety of intensity of pigment creates a mottled, dimensional look. Virtually inert.

Natural paints

Available online and through specialty retailers. These have a rich and subtle appearance. Ingredients come from vegetable and plant-based material but still contain some solvents. Safe once the paint has cured.

Whitewash and milk (casein) paint

Available online and through specialty retailers. Made up of limestone and milk mixed with chalk, linseed oil, and egg, these give a very flat appearance. They require a primer coat for exterior applications. Application is safe, but lime can be a skin irritant. Once cured, virtually inert.

Wallpaper

Available at most hardware and large home stores. Usually made of acrylic (water-based is safer); wheat, starch, cellulose, or clay-based adhesives that stick the "paper" to the wall and can contain chemicals and biocides; a backing layer laminated to the finished surface that is often made from vinyl and off-gasses dangerous compounds. PVC in any part of the product is a known carcinogen, mutagen, and neurotoxin. The solution: avoid vinyl, PVC, chemically enhanced adhesives, and treated wallpaper. Many companies offer responsible, durable, beautiful, and nonsynthetic wallpaper options.

Instant Gratification

Test your paint

Lead-testing kits are sold at hardware stores and are very easy to use on painted surfaces (or on old china and pots).

More Committed?

Before you begin painting any room, start fresh

Remove vinyl or old synthetic wall coverings, if any, and dispose.

The wealth of new low-VOC paint, milk paints, natural plasters, and nontoxic colored glazes will amaze you. You can look to online resources, local faux painters (make sure they know you want a nontoxic, healthy finish), or just visit your local paint store to see what is available. Experiment with layered looks, stamped patterns, hand-painted details, stencils, borders, and unusual application tools. Sponged paint needn't look forced if you apply two or three layers of paint in similar colors with blended edges.

You can get creative with wall finishes once you have found a base product such as a pure matte paint that you are sure is nontoxic. Try adding texture from unexpected sources to your paint. Cinnamon added to a rusty ochre paint richens the color and enlivens the surface. Brown paper grocery bags can be layered on the wall like papier-mâché and finished with wax to give an unusual rustic warmth to an office space or study. Be sure that the glues, binders, and finishes you use are appropriate for the finish and that you are not introducing materials that will harbor moisture or encourage pests. Ribbon trims and anything you can dream up can excite your imagination to look at your walls in an entirely new light!

Cover your walls

Beautifully textured wallpapers from green wall-covering companies are now readily available and made from grasses, linens, and other natural fibers. Be sure the backing, glue, and other binding materials are nontoxic as well.

A Truly Healthy Home

Try your hand at plaster

All sorts of plaster finishes are available, including old-world Venetian plaster (that has bits of marble or limestone in the mix to give it the unique luster and variation found in traditional European country homes and castles). Natural earth-base plaster is the healthiest wall finish and can look very elegant with a waxed finish. The products available to the average do-it-yourselfer range from a crushed-stone powder that gives an Italian villa feel to an integral color clay plaster that reminds one of Southwest adobe finishes.

Research nontoxic plaster materials and finishes until you find what gives you the most peace of mind with your desired look. Get a little advice or encouragement from a local artisan or faux painter and then have fun.

Plaster Ideas to Experiment With at Home

A multitude of tutorials online can help you better understand the ancient process of creating a plaster finish on your walls. Your local paint store may have classes or manufacturer brochures that give you step-by-step instructions, which will vary with each product. Smooth walls are your best starting point, so a newly drywalled room with a smooth finish is ideal (i.e., the "mud" that smooths the seams is not textured to hide flaws). If smooth texture is not an option, rough up the texture in your walls and be prepared to add an extra coat of plaster for a more refined look.

Typically two to three coats are needed to create an old-world feel, but experiment in a small space so you can complete the job! Certain paints and pigments added to a slightly thinner plaster will create a luscious effect. Often a finished plaster wall is burnished (rubbed down with a slightly abrasive material) to give a wall the sheen and look of stone.

Energy & Air Quality

Resources can be conserved via good design, such as sun-exposed windows in winter, or ventilation and shade from awnings, screens, and trees in summer. Faulty seals and poor weather stripping on windows and doors create a need for more heating and cooling. You want your house to breathe, but intentional ventilation design works better than the gaps that lose heat or let cold snaps or heat waves find their way inside. Plus, strategic planning can also improve your home's air quality at the same time.

Window Coverings

Exterior awnings and window overhangs, interior curtains, blinds, and shades help to control temperature. Avoid vinyl or other synthetic, off-gassing materials, and look for designs that minimize dust buildup. Bamboo and paper or organic fabric roll-up shades offer the appeal of simplicity. Wood blinds are beautiful, but be careful to avoid ones from unsustainably harvested rain-forest sources—ask suppliers and let them know your concerns.

Wood Heat

Wood fires are no longer legal in some areas because of air pollution problems. Be aware that wood smoke is a contributing factor in global warming. If you do have wood fires, use only dry wood and avoid damped-down smoldering fires. Use dry, cleaner-burning hardwood if you must use regular firewood, but think twice. Oak makes fine firewood, but far too many oak trees and oak woodland habitats are being lost to development and other causes. Have your chimney inspected and cleaned (once a year); have cracks repaired (they can cause drafts that force unclean air back into the living space or pose a fire danger).

Air Quality

Throughout this book you'll learn about many sources of indoor air pollution that can be avoided. Air filtration methods can be employed if you want to take steps beyond avoiding or removing as many materials as possible that are air pollution sources (such as formaldehyde insulation).

Radiant heating tends to be better than forced-air because it does not blow dusty air around. If you do have forced-air heating, you can do several things to improve the quality of the air. Add a pleated media filter of at least MERV 10 (the rating system used on filters) to a forced-air furnace. Heat exchangers can be added on to the furnace to electrostatically remove dust and dirt from the air. A small electric air filter can be plugged in and placed in bedrooms or individual areas where you want to clean the air.

Air Filter Types

- Mechanical whole-house filtration

- Filters on your heating system (at the intake, at the furnace itself, and at the vents in each room)

- Freestanding HEPA (High Efficiency Particulate Air) filter units

- Ozone-creating devices

- UV filters

NOTE: Fans that draw air from a problem area need an alternative source of fresh replacement air.

Make sure your filters are changed on schedule, and filtration systems serviced and cleaned regularly.

Do all you can to conserve energy resources. Also be aware of the source of your power from the street and check the safety of your electricity (especially after a storm or if you are having any unusual occurrences in the home such as appliances shorting out or acting erratically). Your local power company will usually check your home for free. A safety check from the local utility will help locate dangerous situations and save on wasted power, and if they offer a free energy audit, you can save money as well. Have the service person show you how to determine if there is a problem with your power source, how to turn off the main power and gas, and also how to safely relight a pilot light. Some independent organizations or companies may be useful if you want to learn more about the power pole outside of your home (or you can use the gauss meter, which is a device designed to measure levels of electromagnetic fields, for this) and how to shield yourself from excess electrical fields.

Healthy Construction

If you are building or remodeling, investigate water supply concepts like copper pipe, filtration, and gray-water systems; energy efficiency; solar energy; and green building methods, including straw bale, rammed earth, and eco-sensitive prefabs.

Instant Gratification

Keep warm

Buy clean-burning pellets or use manufactured logs made from recycled wax cardboard instead of commercial varieties that use petroleum additives and don't burn as cleanly.

Keep cool

Set your thermostat at 55 degrees when you are sleeping or not at home in the winter and at 75 degrees in the summer when you are home.

More Committed?

Insulate and weather-strip

For improved energy conservation, insulate vulnerable areas with a nontoxic insulation product. Areas especially prone to energy waste are the roof and attic. Install an automatic attic fan to help control summer heat.

Renew the weather stripping on your doors and windows, but research and buy nontoxic material and adhesives.

Have your furnace and water heater inspected for energy efficiency as well as safety; consider replacing them with energy-conserving models.

Quit smoking

Besides the obvious health benefits for you and your lungs, quitting smoking helps the air quality of your home.

A Truly Healthy Home

May the sun shine

Wise house siting in the architectural phases of planning and landscaping in collaboration with elements such as winter sun and summer breezes is the best start toward comfort and resource conservation. Deciduous trees near south-facing windows help regulate a comfortable climate inside your home environment.

"Bake out" chemicals

Some air quality specialists have looked to the process of off-gassing as a means to find solutions to problems created by household chemicals. If your home is newly constructed or if you have just installed new flooring or painted a room (with nontoxic or regular paint), you can speed the process that releases chemical fumes from these new materials. These gases will be released into the air of your home, so it is crucial to do this carefully. You will need to create a very large amount of air exchange to properly receive the benefits from heating up the materials. Do this when you and your pets are out of the home but not far away—or ask a neighbor or your contractor to monitor the house. Set your thermostat higher than normal for several hours at a time over several weeks but keep the windows wide open and your house ventilation system running. Service your furnace and house filters just before and after doing this to be sure those systems are operating as efficiently as possible. It may seem like an extreme measure, but if you have just purchased a home that is newly constructed or have finished a remodel, it could mean a dramatic difference in air quality and your long-term health. A qualified environmental specialist can help guide you through this process if you are especially sensitive to a new home.

CHAPTER 2

Kitchens

As the world outside gets busier and more complicated, the more we seek ways to nurture ourselves and create a sense of calm and safety at home.

The kitchen, a source of nourishment and bounty, is the place where we go to cook, to eat, and to gather around the kitchen table to talk about the day's events. The most inviting kitchens don't just offer clean, uncluttered spaces and lots of clear light, but entice us with the fragrance of fresh-baked cookies, rich, simmering stews, and the aroma of just-brewed coffee. The good food and nurturing that spring from a healthy kitchen can form the warm heart of your home, welcoming friends and family alike.

Your food, storage methods, and kitchen tools all contribute to the health of your home and your body. Did you know that a cast-iron pan can help provide your body with necessary iron, or that stainless steel thermoses are much healthier than plastic bottles for carrying water?

Food

Western cultures began to consume processed and refined foods in the mid-twentieth century. Today's massive grocery stores were once unheard of. In other times (and still in other countries) people would buy meat from the butcher, produce from the vegetable stand or greengrocer, and baked goods from the bakery. Wherever you buy food, look for organic or pesticide-free (unsprayed), fresh, and locally grown or raised. Time spent at your community's farmers' market is life-affirming.

Government agencies and nutritionists make recommendations about the health benefits of a high-fiber, low-fat diet. Acclaimed healers and "health food" devotees have long promoted a diet of less refined food. A return to simpler and more natural ways of eating makes sense. Our bodies are designed and equipped to process food in its most natural state. We have built-in sensors to tell us when to eat and how much. Eating slowly, savoring your food and chewing it fully, helps your body to digest and obtain nutrients more efficiently. Create delicious meals from unrefined whole grains, fruits and vegetables, lean protein from easily digestible sources, and a balance of fats from vegetable sources for a powerful way to maintain good health.

The importance of food as pleasure should not be forgotten either! Interesting flavors, artful presentation, gratefulness for bounty, and the joy of sharing a wholesome, nutritious meal together with others are all valuable aspects of food.

Organic Food

The problems of industrial agriculture methods include waste and contamination of water, unhealthy chemicals, pesticides, antibiotics and hormones, genetically modified organisms (GMOs), soil depletion and erosion, loss of wildlife habitat, and the dilemma that animals are not always treated humanely. Organic farmers are interested in food purity, water and soil conservation, and preserving diversity in agriculture, an approach that is beneficial to all living systems. The sense of small farmers connecting with the community is at the heart of the organic foods movement. To protect yourself and your family, and to help decrease the demand for chemical pesticides, be sure these foods are grown organically: baby food, strawberries, rice, grains, dairy and animal products, corn, bananas, green beans, peaches, and apples.

Simplified Food Labels for Healthier Eating

Some food labels have little or no meaning. "Natural" tends to mean little unless grouped with specific labels. "Low fat" can also be misleading because it may just be a lower fat version of a product that is very high in fat. Governments and organizations are working to improve labeling systems and food packaging claims, but research this for yourself and you will see it is a confusing subject! Here are some basic labels that you should be looking for to improve the health of your food. Keep in mind, traces of chemicals and contaminants are still found in many products with these labels, so the closer you can examine and get to know your food source, the better. As many toxins and contaminants are fat-soluble, they tend to accumulate in our fat and in the fat of the animals we eat, so eating higher on the food chain increases our potential exposure to toxins that have built up in the ecosystem. Reducing your overall fat intake and personal body fat can reduce your exposure to contaminants and help your body eliminate toxins.

Conventional

Some problems with conventional foods are industrial pesticides, irradiation, fertilizers from toxic sludge and other waste, artificial colors, flavors, and preservatives. Bioengineering, growth hormones, and antibiotics are promoted to produce greater quantities of food, but the environmental and health issues may endanger future generations. Most conventional food growers use synthetic fertilizers, chemicals, preservatives, and pesticides in the growth of the crops. Animals and livestock tend to be more crowded, less humanely treated. Bacteria tainting is more likely in overcrowded, unsanitary conditions. (If you want to substitute some animal products with soy products, be sure that the soy is organic, not genetically modified and not overly processed or packaged. Mass-produced meat products come from a multitude of unsavory sources, so try to limit your intake of processed meats and dairy.)

Free-range/cage free

This may only mean animals have access to an area outside the cage, whether or not they use it is another matter. A local farmers' market touting free-range/cage-free eggs or poultry may be more likely to actually have chickens that get fed a diverse diet and roam outside. Eggs tend to take on the flavor of the chicken feed, and most chefs agree that a free-range, organic egg tastes better. Again, if you can visit the farm and see how the animal lives, all the better!

GMO (Genetically Modified Organism)

You won't see this on the label, but most conventionally grown foods are potentially GMOs. This is common in grains, especially soybeans for many products and in grains for livestock feed. Modifying plants to make them resistant to chemicals is highly criticized by scientists, environmentalists, and ecologists. How GMOs affect our health is still unknown.

Organic

No pesticides are used in the growing process, but if grown near conventional crops, organics can have traces of pesticides, so wash even prewashed greens. Most synthetic (and petroleum-derived) pesticides and fertilizers, and all antibiotics, genetic engineering, irradiation, and sewage sludge are prohibited for use in organic production. In addition, organic animals must eat 100 percent organic feed that does not contain any animal by-products or growth hormones. Organic animals also must have access to the outdoors, but chickens are not required to go outside to be organic.

Wild vs. farmed fish and mercury levels

Farmed fish are typically exposed to antibiotics and fed colored pellets to make their flesh look more appetizing. Nonnative species can escape their farms and pose threats to ecosystems. High levels of mercury are a potential health issue when eating fish. Many organizations monitor mercury levels in fish; check their Web sites for the latest news on what seafood currently has low levels of mercury and is harvested sustainably. Children, and women who are pregnant or nursing, are most vulnerable to the effects of mercury poisoning.

Certified humane/free farmed

Guarantees a humane and clean environment for animals used for food. "Animal Care Certified" is not as stringent and means little in terms of what an average person considers humane (for instance chickens only require an 8-by-11-inch space). Antibiotics can be used to treat sick animals.

The Meal as a Sacred Ritual

Take pride in the preparation and presentation, and experience the value of food as nourishment and a means of overall health and balance. Try to set regular times for eating at the table as a family, sharing stories and socializing. Select beautiful serving dishes or create place settings from a mixture of old and new plates and bowls. Use old dishes as a way to honor the past and combine with something new as a way to lend inspiration for the future. (Buy a simple lead-test kit available from most hardware stores to test the glaze on antique dishes that you use for food.) Eat meals from different cultures, shop locally, and encourage your grocery store to stock food from local sources. Visit these sources and find out about the way they produce the food. Find out about pesticides, fertilizer, shipping methods. Eat fresh foods in season: they taste better and are produced using fewer resources.

Bulk Food, Healthy Snacks

Buy in bulk from a reputable whole-food store or grocer who can tell you the direct source of the food. Buying bulk foods reduces waste and cost.

Create an organized system for your pantry and a regular shopping list that includes the purchase of more natural and bulk foods, keeping healthy foods on hand for preparing meals and snacking. Make healthy snacks accessible to kids in clear containers and educate them about the importance of well-rounded meals and snacks that provide nutrition and energy (for running faster, dancing more beautifully, and growing strong and healthy). Help your kids understand so that they create lifelong positive eating habits. This will also benefit them later in life when pressures of junk food and fun packaging tempt.

Instant Gratification

Meal planning

If you are not already choosing organic foods for most of your meals, start planning at least one meal a week that is completely natural and organic. Consider the way many famous chefs cook, which is inspired by whatever locally grown, in-season produce looks and tastes the best. Keep it simple and prepare foods that fit your mood.

Create a recipe box or scrapbook of new organic and healthy meal ideas

Pick up a copy of the newsletter or flyer from your favorite health food store for inspirational recipe ideas. Copy or tear out recipes from cooking magazines and start a three-ring binder of some favorites. Make the book or recipe box an artful project so that it encourages you to open and add to it. You can use regular laundry starch to paste colorful images of food, table settings, or dinner parties on the exterior of the box or binder.

Buy an inspiring cookbook

Spend a quiet afternoon at your local bookstore. Peruse colorful cookbooks with recipes based on fresh, seasonal ingredients for inspiration, or learn about the cuisines of other cultures.

Experiment with old standbys

Sometimes a simple recipe will call for additions that you can vary depending on your preferences, and that recipe can become your own. Modification and experimentation may lead to unusual variations and a tastier, healthier treat once you know how to work with nutritious additions and substitutions. For a standard cookie recipe, opt for organic chocolate chips, organic rolled oats, whole wheat flour, organic/free-range/vitamin-enriched eggs, rich and dark organic brown sugar, sustainably harvested high mineral content sea salt (also great for the bath), organic butter or organic and healthy butter substitutes (usually made from olive oil), even a local baker's organic toffee bits.

Change your pet food (and flea soap)

Don't forget the family pet when you begin to shift your buying habits at the grocery store. Many commercially available pet foods are made from meat by-products unfit for human consumption. Pesticides, additives, and other unknowns can be found in many pet foods. Flea collars, shampoos, bombs, and powders are all toxic poisons. Try natural alternatives such as eucalyptus oil or pods attached to a collar. Adding brewer's yeast to pets' food can help with fleas, as will clove and citrus oil rubbed on their fur.

More Committed?

Visit your local farmers' market

While you can still find roadside fruit and produce stands in more rural areas, farmers' markets have become popular throughout suburban and city communities. Find out where your market suppliers grow their food and how it gets to you. Talk to the growers at the market, because they know more about their product than anyone else. While many farmers' markets do not always sell products at reduced prices, supporting a small farm can help to connect you to food in ways that buying at a grocery chain cannot. You are enabling this provider to maintain a livelihood that nurtures and supports your family as well.

Join a food group

Become involved in your community's food sources by joining a local farm cooperative, produce-buying club, or community group that supports local food growers.

Find out about the chemicals in your food

You can do this easily by searching online. An example of food additives that you should know about is perchlorate. Found in milk and lettuce, it is linked to impaired thyroid function, tumors, cancer, and decreased learning capacity and developmental problems around hearing and speech.

A Truly Healthy Home

Support local farmers

Take your kids to visit a local organic farm or producer and then a large factory-type food-production facility to see the differences in where your food comes from. Make it a family field trip or organize your child's school to visit local food resources. If you don't know of any local growers, ask your grocery store if they buy from any local suppliers and try to set up a field trip. Ask questions of the owners of these food sources: are they using chemicals, pesticides, or antibiotics? Are the facilities clean (especially beef and dairy)? Educating yourself about the actual practices and beliefs of the farmer you support is a crucial step in finding and maintaining healthy food sources.

Bake bread from scratch or in a bread maker

The smell is like no other! If you have the time to bake bread from scratch, kneading the dough and letting it rise get you back in touch with a simple process of understanding how time nurtures everything. It may even inspire you to nurture yourself. Get back in touch with your own natural cycle for rest, contemplation, and creativity.

Start an organic herb garden in a window

A window herb garden—outside in a window box or inside on a sunlit sill—is a great way to start reaping the benefits of homegrown flavor. Herbs that do well in a sunny window and have many savory and health-promoting uses are basil, garlic, chives, cilantro, oregano, and parsley. Freshly chopped herbs add a special touch to any dish.

Grow your own organic veggies

If you are lucky to have the space and energy to grow some of your own veggies, you can start small with a potted tomato plant or a simple square of soil to try a few varieties. Certain plants will grow better in your particular climate and it's best to try different vegetables to see what thrives. Be sure your soil is uncontaminated and that added fertilizer or mulch is organic and natural, and any pest deterrents are safe, nontoxic, and organic (soapy sprays that repel many types of insects with no dangerous residue are sold at most garden stores). Learn more about this in chapter 7, "The Great Outdoors."

Water

Water Quality and Filtration

Because water is so essential to our health, it makes sense that the quality of the water we consume is a matter of great importance. Municipal water uses chlorine or chlorine dioxide to disinfect the drinking water supply. Water is one of the world's best solvents, and adding chemicals to water spreads them quickly and can be harmful. The chemical combination of these treatment additives and many types of water pipes (such as PVC or degrading heavy metals) can be even more dangerous. To reap the health benefits of water, you'll want to ensure the water you put in your body is fresh, pure, clean, and delicious.

You can use a simple freestanding water filter pitcher or install a faucet mount. Filtration for your drinking water is important, but keeping the filters clean and determining which filter is best for your particular situation are also crucial.

Assess Your Water Quality

Your local water department must provide information about the quality of your water, but understanding these reports (often in a newsletter format) can be tricky. As water departments must regularly meet drinking water standards, it seems there should be no reason for concern. But who sets these standards and what kind of studies are being done about low-level exposures to chemicals over long-term periods? Because these chemicals also break down into other compounds when mixed with air or the ingredients of your pipes, it is hard to determine exactly the quality of water that is coming out of your tap. Several independent companies sell testing kits: collect a sample of your water and send it to a lab. Be aware that an individual testing company may be more objective than someone selling you something. Never lose sight of the fact that being armed with the knowledge of what's in your water can help you to keep yourself and your family safe.

Appliances

Gas

Gas appliances are one of the most common sources of preventable indoor air pollution. If they are not properly installed, serviced, or vented, your gas appliances can give off gases, including carbon monoxide, nitrogen dioxide, nitrous oxide, and even small amounts of formaldehyde. Models with a constantly burning pilot light are not as healthy as ones with an electronic ignition because the noxious fumes will be released in small amounts all the time.

Vent your gas appliances such as a gas stove top, if you have one. It is crucial to supply replacement air whenever you use the vent. This prevents negative pressure from building up and drawing air from the easiest source, which may be your fireplace flue or other unclean source. If you are unsure if your ventilation system supplies replacement air, just open a window when you cook. Have your utility provider or a licensed HVAC professional inspect your gas stove and furnace to determine if you have any gas leaks and to be sure your ventilation system is working safely.

Electric

All electric appliances produce electromagnetic fields (EMFs) whether they are on or off, unless unplugged. Always exercise caution and common sense when operating electrical appliances. Keep all of your kitchen appliances clean and free of food debris. Your choice of cleaning product is especially important here as it will get heated and re-release fumes or it will come in direct contact with your food. As for self-cleaning ovens, the materials and coatings on these types of ovens are toxic, especially when heated, so use the self-cleaning cycle sparingly or not at all.

Microwave

Studies on the safety of microwave ovens are controversial. Many reports have shown that the basic structure of the food is altered when heated in a microwave. One study showed that the immune-system-enhancing quality of breast milk was reduced during microwaving by the breakdown of certain antibodies and proteins. Some of the most frightening studies to date note the dangers of heating plastics in the microwave, especially if the food in the plastic container has any fat in it. The combination of fat, high heat, and plastics releases dioxin into the food and ultimately into the cells of the body.

If you must use a microwave, limit its use, especially for food for infants and children, and stand as far away from it as possible during use. Have the microwave checked for leakage and never use plastic containers or plastic wrap: use heat-safe glass or microwave-safe ceramic containers for heating food.

Dioxins

Dioxins are a group of hazardous by-products from a range of chemical, manufacturing, and combustion processes. Extremely tiny doses of dioxin have been shown to cause negative health effects. Studies have linked dioxins to many types of cancer as well as to reproductive problems, abnormalities in fetal development, immune-system alterations, and disruption of hormones. Because dioxins are attracted to fat and are resistant to metabolism, they are notorious for accumulating in the animals humans eat, and by that route accumulating in humans. Within the human body, the highest levels of these chemicals are in fat and breast milk.

Cookware

Innovations in cookware, including the use of less expensive metals and new nonstick finishes, have brought us some health scares that are worth considering. Some of the pots and pans available today in high-end department stores are expensive, beautiful, and well designed, but the materials used to make them could be a source of concern. Aluminum has been suspected as a link to Alzheimer's disease. Teflon as a surface coating in cookware is a concern because of PFCs (perfluorochemicals), which have been found to be harmful when tested on animals. Because there are so many perfectly safe alternatives to nonstick cookware, it is a good idea to phase out your use of these items.

Discard your nonstick pans, especially any that are old, pitted, or scratched. If you can't part with a favorite omelette pan, be sure that you do not overheat it, as the compound perfluorooctanoic acid (PFOA) should not pose a problem if the pan is never heated beyond the medium setting.

Use clay, stainless steel, ceramic, glass, porcelain, or cast-iron cookware. One of the advantages of cast iron is that it can actually provide small amounts of iron, which is a necessary nutrient in the human diet. Silicon used in cookware seems inert, but it is a newer product with less long-term health analysis.

Vintage dishware can lend a wonderful look to your table, but only if you cautiously evaluate the condition of your ceramics. Many glazes contain harmful lead and should not be used for food service. Also beware of cracked glazes that can harbor bacteria. Retire dangerous dishware from your kitchen and instead display them on plate hangers or on a high shelf.

Food Packaging & Storage

Dioxin, other carcinogens, and hormone-disrupting phthalates are associated with the use of plastic. The softer plastics (including those used in children's toys) are made pliable by the use of phthalates. These chemicals have been linked to nerve disruption and immune-system problems. People with sensitized immune systems or developing endocrine systems, pregnant women, newborns, and young children, are most at risk from the dangers of plastics. It is very difficult to properly clean plastic to be sure that it is free of bacteria, and if it is washed sufficiently, such cleaning breaks down and releases the chemicals that are damaging to our health.

Use glass for food and water storage, or use stainless steel thermoses for carrying liquids. Consider a switch to glass or lightweight stainless steel containers to pack children's (or grown-ups') lunches to eliminate the need for plastics and to reduce waste—vintage metal lunch boxes are available online, and vintage and new metal thermoses are common. Cornstarch packaging for take away food is becoming available.

It is easy to make your own padded carrying case for a small glass water bottle. Carrying water will help you stay hydrated while driving around, working, and doing errands. Keep in mind that a too-large bottle may get too heavy. For a carrying case, you can use old upholstery fabric, remnants of fabric from a fabric store, burlap, old jeans—try to reuse something old or buy fabric that is from an organic fabric supplier and is free of chemicals and finishing agents.

To prevent food poisoning from bacteria or allergies from mold, don't leave food out on the counter too long. Keep your grains and pantry foods stored in glass containers that have rubber seals or in glass jars in the refrigerator. Rotate—use and replace—stored foods and emergency supplies.

Buying foods in bulk sidesteps the problem of extraneous packaging. For storage, try stainless steel, vintage and new glass refrigerator ware—glass jars work fine, too. Food-storage and composting bags made of starches from vegetable sources have become available. These are better for our health and the environment and create less waste. When you shop for produce, use paper bags when you can and practice paper reuse and recycling. A canvas or net market bag produces zero waste.

Plastics by number

Polyethylene terephthalate (PET)

Soda and water containers, some water-proof packaging. Not recommended for reuse because difficult to clean and remove bacterial contamination. Proper cleaning releases more chemicals. This type of plastic may also leach DEHA, a known carcinogen, when reused.

High-density polyethylene

Milk, detergent, oil bottles. Toys and plastic bags. Less toxic than many other plastics.

Vinyl/polyvinyl chloride (PVC)

Food wrap, vegetable oil bottles, blister packages. Made flexible by use of phthalates (suspected carcinogen) and dioxin (known carcinogen) released during manufacturing and incineration.

Low-density polyethylene

Many plastic bags, shrink wrap, garment bags. Less toxic than many other plastics.

Polypropylene

Refrigerated containers, some bags, most bottle tops, some carpets, some food wrap. Considered safest.

Polystyrene

Throwaway utensils, meat packaging, protective packing. Known to cause functional impairment of the nervous system. Styrene is a carcinogen and mutagen, highly toxic, and may be leached into foods contained in polystyrene.

Other

Usually layered or mixed plastic. No recycling potential, must be landfilled.

Plastic labeled 7 is LEXAN or polycarbonate plastic and is used in water bottles purchased from sporting goods stores and in industry. Bisphenol A (BPA), linked to chromosome abnormalities in mice, chromosome damage, and hormone disruption, can leach harmful chemicals into the water.

Kitchen Design

The kitchen of the ideal Healthy Home is designed to take advantage of good natural light for improved visibility (and less need for artificial lighting). You really need to see what you are doing in the kitchen. If you are building a kitchen, you can get the most from natural sunlight by orienting your kitchen according to your priorities (east for early-morning people, south for colder climates, and west for the person who spends afternoons and evenings in the kitchen). Ventilation from open windows and cross breezes should be a part of the design as well (you can add mechanical ventilation). Window coverings help with privacy and control brightness. If natural light from windows is hard to come by, skylights or Solatubes are a great way to add light without direct sun exposure.

Nontoxic construction materials and finishes, healthy shopping habits, and food quality all contribute to a beneficial environment. The materials you bring into this space are often more problematic than you might think, but small changes can start a cascading effect of enlightenment!

Plastics by number

Polyethylene terephthalate (PET)

Soda and water containers, some waterproof packaging. Not recommended for reuse because difficult to clean and remove bacterial contamination. Proper cleaning releases more chemicals. This type of plastic may also leach DEHA, a known carcinogen, when reused.

High-density polyethylene

Milk, detergent, oil bottles. Toys and plastic bags. Less toxic than many other plastics.

Vinyl/polyvinyl chloride (PVC)

Food wrap, vegetable oil bottles, blister packages. Made flexible by use of phthalates (suspected carcinogen) and dioxin (known carcinogen) released during manufacturing and incineration.

Low-density polyethylene

Many plastic bags, shrink wrap, garment bags. Less toxic than many other plastics.

Polypropylene

Refrigerated containers, some bags, most bottle tops, some carpets, some food wrap. Considered safest.

Polystyrene

Throwaway utensils, meat packaging, protective packing. Known to cause functional impairment of the nervous system. Styrene is a carcinogen and mutagen, highly toxic, and may be leached into foods contained in polystyrene.

Other

Usually layered or mixed plastic. No recycling potential, must be landfilled.

Plastic labeled 7 is LEXAN or polycarbonate plastic and is used in water bottles purchased from sporting goods stores and in industry. Bisphenol A (BPA), linked to chromosome abnormalities in mice, chromosome damage, and hormone disruption, can leach harmful chemicals into the water.

Baby bottles are made from polyethylene (also known as EVA plastics) and polycarbonate. Do not heat formula or breast milk in plastic bottles! *Never* microwave plastic baby bottles (not only because of what it may do to the plastic, but because it creates hot spots that could burn your baby's mouth) or any plastic food containers; it is just not worth the risk. There is concern that bisphenol-A leaches into the liquid when heated. If you must use plastic baby bottles, heat the formula separately or transfer the breast milk just before giving it to your child and discard the leftover. To be extra safe, use glass bottles.

Cleaning

Most people keep a variety of cleaning products under the kitchen sink and use them throughout the house. The chemicals found in most conventional cleaning products are not only noxious but have been found to be very toxic. Consider that food preparation occurs on surfaces cleaned with many of these products, which means you may be eating these chemicals! Because household cleaning products pose such a threat to a Healthy Home, an entire section at the end of this book is devoted to cleaning (see pages 169–76). There you will better understand the most widely used chemicals in most traditional cleaning products and find safer and more gentle alternatives to use everywhere in your home.

Recycling & Composting

Recycling

Recycling makes you more aware of the packaging that you purchase and discard. If you take responsibility for every type of waste you create and become more aware of what items can be reused, or truly recycled back into the product it starts out as (such as glass bottles becoming new glass bottles), you may find yourself purchasing fewer items that use nonrecyclable packaging. Once you start to understand how plastics, in particular, stay in the environment, you may use them less often and possibly expose yourself to fewer chemicals. People who sort their own recyclables tend to have a higher recycling rate and less garbage in general because of the tendency to be more tuned in to the process of creating and disposing of waste.

Start recycling. Many cities offer curbside recycling programs; if yours doesn't, consider asking for one. Plan a field trip to your local dump or garbage processing and recycling center.

Learn about the number system applied to plastics from the recycling system codes mentioned in the sidebar on page 59. It's helpful to know what health hazards exist for each plastic type, but your purchasing habits might also be affected by understanding what gets recycled, down-cycled (plastic containers that aren't recyclable get turned into a new product and eventually discarded), and dropped in a landfill.

Composting

If you're willing, try composting—it really connects you to the cycle of nature and vastly reduces the waste going to the landfill. If you have a "green waste" day in your neighborhood, you can use vegetable starch–based garbage bags, but it is still best to use the large container instead of garbage bags. If you have a garden, compost is a treasure for amending your soil. Even if you don't have a garden, get a worm box for composting kitchen scraps from fruits and vegetables, and give the castings to a gardening friend. If your community's recycling service doesn't provide for collection of compostables, be a thorn in its side until it does. A Healthy Home is connected to nature and to its community, so community composting is the way to start.

Kitchen Design

The kitchen of the ideal Healthy Home is designed to take advantage of good natural light for improved visibility (and less need for artificial lighting). You really need to see what you are doing in the kitchen. If you are building a kitchen, you can get the most from natural sunlight by orienting your kitchen according to your priorities (east for early-morning people, south for colder climates, and west for the person who spends afternoons and evenings in the kitchen). Ventilation from open windows and cross breezes should be a part of the design as well (you can add mechanical ventilation). Window coverings help with privacy and control brightness. If natural light from windows is hard to come by, skylights or Solatubes are a great way to add light without direct sun exposure.

Nontoxic construction materials and finishes, healthy shopping habits, and food quality all contribute to a beneficial environment. The materials you bring into this space are often more problematic than you might think, but small changes can start a cascading effect of enlightenment!

Instant Gratification

Get some fresh air

Open the window when you are cooking or using the appliances in your kitchen. Keep countertops uncluttered and clean, and wipe up spills and crumbs on a regular basis. Be sure to use nontoxic cleaning products and rags that can be washed. Sponges harbor germs and molds even when rinsed thoroughly.

More Committed?

Save power and water

Purchase new energy-efficient refrigerator, dishwasher, or washer and dryer. Replace old nonoperable windows with double-paned, operable windows to allow you to control temperature.

A Truly Healthy Home

Safe surfaces

Nontoxic building materials such as formaldehyde-free cabinet boxes and doors are available in many styles and color palettes. A truly healthy kitchen will have no major surfaces contaminated with or containing formaldehyde or plastic by-products. Synthetically produced solid-surface countertops are durable and attractive, but it remains to be seen what possible harm could come from the off-gassing of these materials in the future as they wear. Best to play it safe with stone, stone tile, nontoxic concrete, wood, or new solid surfacing materials that are nontoxic and tested for chemical off-gassing. Sealants for these natural materials need to be nontoxic and proven effective.

CHAPTER 3

Bedrooms

Bedrooms

Rest, rejuvenation, and sanctuary are the inspirations for your bedroom.

If you get the eight hours' sleep we need, you spend more time in your bedroom than in any other room in the house. It's the place you go to rest, to dream, to read, to share intimacy—and to maintain optimal health. When you sleep, your brain is busy doing the essential work of fighting disease by producing hormones such as melatonin. Depending on your bedroom environment, such essential restorative processes can be helped or hindered. Light pollution—the lack of true darkness—interferes with the immune system. Poor choice of furniture, linens, mattresses, and dry-cleaning products can turn our dream bedroom into a source of pollutants. Petrochemical materials, fiberboard bound with noxious glues and treated with formaldehyde, synthetic fibers and "wrinkle guard" have been found to cause severe reactions in some individuals and have been linked to hormone disruption. If you are going to select one room in which to be especially picky in terms of furnishings, decoration, and fabric choices, the bedroom is a great place.

There are many things you can do to make your and your family's bedrooms healthier. Some of them are as simple as changing sheets or laundry detergents. Others require a little more time and commitment. But when you consider the hours spent in your bedroom and the importance of the activities that occur there, it's worth a little time spent making it a nurturing and toxic-free place dedicated to contemplation, peace, and dreams.

Design, Layout & Ambience

Some intriguing and ancient philosophies such as Ayurvedic teachings from India and feng shui from China have become popular in today's design practice and literature. These involve special attention to placement, natural elements, geographical directions, and sometimes astrological signs. A major concept is that room orientations, color, furniture layouts, and other factors can either enhance or disrupt your energy and health. The place where you sleep can be an essential focus of these philosophies. Whether feng shui or any other practice holds meaning for you, adopting some of the principles makes good design sense. Keep in mind for your bedroom that in this very personal space what matters is how it makes you feel and that it encourages restfulness and relaxation.

Place personal objects and perhaps a photo of loved ones in this room, but keep it uncluttered and clean. Clutter encourages dust and an overload of visual input, which especially at bedtime can be too stimulating or distracting.

Your Bed

Be sure your bed is up off the floor to encourage air circulation and discourage moisture and stagnancy. If you need a bed frame to raise a futon off the floor, ask a local craftsperson or assemble a simple frame yourself from certified sustainably harvested lumber or salvaged, clean wood from an old structure. Pick a bed design with slatted wood supports; futon frames work well because the slats encourage air circulation. Choose solid wood with nontoxic finishes and no pesticides or formaldehyde glues. Slatted wood support systems exist in most antique beds. You can find a beautiful bed at an estate sale or antique store.

Keep a Dream Journal

Dreams can be keys to your inner beliefs, helping you sort through troubling issues or fulfilling a need to escape into fantasy when the stresses of everyday life keep your brain humming all day long. Not only can a dream journal remind you to take time to savor the world of the subconscious that we enter while we sleep, but it may help to get you off to sleep. For those who have trouble falling asleep or who sleep lightly, it may help to have a separate notepad or a special "to do" section in your dream journal where you jot down your day's worries and nagging thoughts. Write down what is bothering you or keeping you awake at night, shut the book, and then tuck it away to prevent troubled thoughts from lingering.

Limit the Negative Effects of Electricity

Electromagnetic fields (EMFs) have become a serious concern. In the bedroom, the simplest way to reduce the negative effects of these fields is to locate your clock radio, air purifiers, baby monitors, and any other electronic devices as far away from your head as possible. Reducing the amount of metal in the bedroom, especially in your bed frame or mattress, can help with problems from electricity. Although metal bed frames are popular and inexpensive, metal tends to intensify electromagnetic fields.

It may help to order a device called a gauss meter to check the levels of EMFs in areas where family members sleep. You can buy one of these devices and share the cost with several friends, who can take turns checking their homes for high levels of EMFs. Don't sleep with an electric blanket, and move cell phone chargers out of the bedroom (unplugging them when not in use). You can have a switch installed that turns off all power to this room while you sleep. Use an old-fashioned wind-up alarm clock and reading lights run on rechargeable batteries (conventional batteries are a major source of toxic pollution).

Colors and Patterns

Everyone has a preferred palette of colors that evokes emotional responses. Spend some time looking at colors as they exist in nature and take note of your reactions to earth-toned browns and beiges, varied greens, and subtle blues and grays. For the bedroom, choose the colors that make you feel the most calm and at peace. If there is wide variation between what you like and what the person who shares your bedroom prefers, think about compromise and opt for neutral beiges and more subtle shades of colors. Variations of one neutral color similar to the shifts in color and light that occur in nature can work to create a calming effect.

Keep the overall decorating theme simple but meaningful. Add interest with texture and opt for patterns inspired by nature, as they tend to have a more grounding and soothing effect. Don't be afraid of mixing and matching bedding from different companies or playing with complementary color palettes and patterns. To prevent this room from feeling monotonous and bland, use touches of brighter, purer colors to liven the space. Red and rose are colors associated with intimacy and romance and can be used in small doses to infuse the bedroom with warmth and love.

Instant Gratification

Sweet dreams

Philosophies may differ: do some research and consider what seems right to you regarding the most beneficial direction to orient of your head while sleeping. Try several furniture arrangements to place your bed in a position that creates the best feeling of security for you. Don't locate your bed under a beam, under windows, or in a place that is too drafty.

Relaxing scents

Add an aromatherapy candle made from beeswax or soy and pick a scent that fits a mood of relaxation or romance such as lavender, ylang-ylang, or jasmine. (Beware of commercial candles made with toxic waxes, wicks containing lead, and artificial scents.)

More Committed?

Calming colors

Select a theme for the bedroom and start to make changes that fit the vision. Use tea, coffee, or other natural dyes to add color to organic cotton sheets. Or buy bedding made from organic cotton grown in a range of natural colors. Have fun working with tints as a way to integrate and calm the bedroom atmosphere.

Inspiring images

Change your art. Take digital photos of natural objects up close and produce your own abstract art. You can use photo software and turn images into duotones or sepia prints to create subtle, artistic renditions of captivating shapes and compositions. Buy frames made of recycled wood and try to use glass, not Plexiglas; old frames from thrift stores can be charming as is or easily reconditioned with a nontoxic finish. Unfortunately many imported, mass-produced wooden frames are by-products of the clear-cutting of exotic woods; investigate before you buy.

A Truly Healthy Home

Healthy home materials

If you are ready to remodel, redecorate, or just update bedrooms, spend some time to learn more about healthy materials and decorating using nontoxic products. Try a natural plaster finish, refurbished vintage or antique furniture (a quality piece of older furniture may need nothing more than a coat of nontoxic wax to spruce it up).

Bedding

Look for unbleached, untreated, and, if possible, organic cottons and linens—they're the best materials for healthy bedding and are widely available. Ordinary cotton is one of the most heavily sprayed crops in agriculture; organic cotton is better for you and the planet. Labels that indicate your bedding is of higher quality include: certified organic cotton, certified organic wool, combed cotton, Egyptian cotton, flannel, percale, pima cotton, pure-finish cotton, Pure Grow Wool, staple, Supima cotton, thread counts of 180 or higher, untreated cotton, and upland cotton. Duvets filled with cotton or wool may be better for those with allergies than down or down plus feathers, certainly better than synthetic fill.

Many conventional sheets are made from polyester-cotton blends and finished with chemicals for a "wrinkle-free" finish. Formaldehyde is the most commonly used chemical to create this finish and has been known to cause headaches, skin rashes, asthma attacks, fatigue, and insomnia. Most mattresses and foam pillows sold in department stores are sprayed with fungicides, pesticides, and flame retardants, the last known to create irreversible damage to children's nervous systems. Foam mattresses and pads made with petroleum products and other chemicals emit toxic fumes that can create allergic responses in some individuals and may present carcinogenic and other health risks. Ask the manufacturer or retail store about materials and processing, and don't be afraid to ask more questions if you don't feel comfortable that you are getting a complete answer.

Assess your bedding and determine which items to replace. You can do this by reading the content labels and by feel. Don't feel pressured to switch everything on your bed overnight. Subtle changes can improve your health dramatically, especially if you determine that you are sensitive to particular materials. Some people are sensitive or allergic to natural materials such as latex, down, or wool (it may be wool itself or the way the material is processed or treated). Down can be allergenic for some; if you choose it for a feather bed, pillows, or duvets, be sure to clean it according to the manufacturer's directions. High-quality down is exceptionally warm and comfortable in many climates because it is light and insulating. Our association of wool with itchy sweaters and strange smells may come from the pesticides, bleaches, or dyes in most commercial wools. High-quality wool is available that is softer and very comfortable for sleeping due to its insulation and moisture-wicking properties.

Wash your bedding frequently, using fragrance-free laundry *soap* (not detergents) with nonpetroleum-based surfactants (sudsing agents that create lather). The product should be chlorine-free (to avoid dioxin toxicity), phosphate-free, and labeled nontoxic and biodegradable. Bedding (and jammies) are close to your skin for long periods of time, so your choices are important here. Switching to gentler detergents and reducing or avoiding bleach are some of the simplest ways to reduce chemical exposure on your body.

Instant Gratification

Warm toes

Electric blankets should not be used because of the high electromagnetic field they create. If you must use an electric blanket to warm a bed, unplug and remove it before climbing in. A hot water bottle placed at the bottom of your bed is a safe and age-old way of warming cold sheets.

Clean feet

Showering or taking a relaxing bath before bed can help you unwind and sleep more restfully. Another advantage to cleansing your body before slipping into bed is that you make sure that accumulated sweat, dirt, and possible chemicals or environmental pollutants that you have been exposed to during the day don't follow you into your bed. This will also keep your sheets cleaner and discourage dust mites.

More Committed?

A good airing

In good weather, take your bedding and mattress outside to air in the sunshine, a great way to purify materials, decrease dust, and discourage dust mites and mold. The smell of fabric aired outdoors can't be beat!

Keep it covered

Purchase pillow and mattress covers to encase your current ones until you can make changes. Even once you have switched to healthier pillows and mattresses, you may want to keep 100 percent organic cotton covers on these items as they decrease the dirt, dust, and skin cells that contaminate the filling, inviting dust mites. Remove and wash covers in hot or warm water weekly using natural laundry soap.

A Truly Healthy Home

Replace your mattress

If your mattress is a conventional polyurethane foam mattress with or without metal coils, consider purchasing a new mattress made from natural materials such as latex foam or cotton or wool batting. Look for mattresses, mattress pads, and futons made from untreated and 100 percent organic fibers. High-quality luxury ones are now available from many online resources, ensuring you years of restful sleep.

Clothing & Closets

Most change starts with a shift in attitude or perceptions. If you find a new way of looking at your buying habits and develop a conscious philosophy about what your clothing and other purchases can represent, you might experience surprising revelations. Personal style and the way you dress are reflections of your beliefs about who you want to be and how you want to be perceived. By shifting your habits toward more natural and high-quality garments, produced by people who care about health, who want to protect the environment and ensure positive working conditions for the people who make your clothes, you're supporting and nurturing an entire cycle of sustainability. There are lots of non-sweatshop clothing companies that promote fair trade, sustainable manufacturing, and healthy material usage. It might take some time to find the right mix of healthy materials and design for your personal style, but it's likely you'll find a company (or even local artisan) whose support from you will not go unnoticed! Many of these companies provide excellent customer service and a personal, cottage-industry style of operating business.

Hidden Secrets

Our closets are metaphors for mysteries we keep, but you may not know how many environmentally toxic secrets they may hold. Synthetic materials are culprits, plus we gather chemical residues on our clothing due to what we have been exposed to during our day. Your closet encloses clothing, shoes, and sometimes freshly dry-cleaned garments that bring some of the most toxic pollutants into the home environment.

Shoes are hosts for residues of landscaping pesticides, urban grime from petro- and other chemicals, and moisture (conducive to mold). Clothing absorbs cigarette smoke, other toxic chemicals, and odors. These pollutants stay in the fabric and begin to release back into the air of your home. Designate a good place to air out the day's shoes and any clothes that aren't headed straight for the laundry basket. Store well-aired shoes in closed cubbies or raised off the floor to keep pesticide residues, chemicals, and dirt off of your closet floor.

Even the fabric that makes up many of our garments can give off noxious fumes. Polyester fleece is popular because the fabric repels moisture and because it can be produced from recycled bottles and made into snuggly clothing. However, this material has been known to continue to off-gas potentially harmful fumes long after it has been washed many times. The most common worrisome chemicals in synthetic fabrics are benzene, ammonia, and ethylene glycol. These chemicals have known side effects such as depression of the central nervous system, irritation of the eyes, nose, and throat, and links to leukemia, tumors, and cancer. Keep this in mind for your toddler whose pj's or outdoor outfits are often made of fuzzy, warm "fleece." Fabric made from recycled (down-cycled) soda bottles is not any different and, in fact, might encourage use of plastic food containers as new markets for plastic waste are created.

New clothing is often treated with fabric finishes, sizing chemicals, and fire retardants. All of these chemicals are toxic; washing your new clothing immediately after purchase can help reduce toxicity, but it's better to look for truly natural-fiber, untreated clothes.

The dry-cleaning process is really a liquid dip of toxic chemicals that stay in your clothing for months if not longer. Dry-cleaning businesses themselves are a cause of air pollution. If you have outfits you must dry-clean, be sure to let them air outdoors before you bring them inside, and don't store them in your bedroom. The plastic cover over your clothing is also impregnated with the toxic chemicals and should be removed and left at the cleaner's.

A growing number of "green" dry cleaners are popping up, but be sure to ask first what they use, how they handle your clothing, and what other operations occur at the facility. It is much better to launder your own clothing so that you know what products are being used. Clothes labeled "dry-clean only" can often be laundered in a cold water wash and laid flat to dry. This includes wool sweaters, silk, and nonstructured clothing. If all else fails, at least close your closet door when possible until you can make significant changes in your buying habits.

Instant Gratification

L'armoire

If you don't have a formal closet, store clothing in a zippered canvas "armoire" or a wooden armoire with a door that closes.

Change from plastic or metal to wooden hangers

Wood that is finished with nontoxic sealant is the safest material for hangers. You can find vintage wooden hangers. Fabric-covered hangers that have been laundered are good for garments that slip easily or become stretched out after hanging. Metal should be kept to a minimum in bedrooms, so try to give these hangers to a local laundromat or dry cleaner.

More Committed?

Clean out your closet!

Go through your closet and remove any item that doesn't fit, isn't flattering, or is outdated. Appraise worn-out clothes for potential for camping, gardening, or material for cleaning rags. Before total rejection, determine whether removed items hold hope of embellishing or altering to give them new life. This culling should be something you do on a regular basis. It could be helpful to get a friend or loved one to sit down with you and help tackle this project. Donate your clothing to an organization of your choice and resist the urge to buy more (at least for now!). This will give you more space and is a good start toward a future of healthier buying habits. Being particular about what you buy can have a dramatic impact on the health of your clothing, and it starts with understanding what you really need and love.

Almost a purist

If you've already thinned out your closet and removed the obvious items, you can take the next step and begin to look at your clothing based on their fiber content. Start with the items that you wear directly on your skin such as undergarments, T-shirts, and socks. Try to keep cotton and other nonsynthetic materials only. Some fibers such as nylon and Lycra are blended with cotton and linen or hemp to make them perform better—these may stay in your wardrobe for a while, until you become more familiar with the many options available from entirely natural and nontoxic materials.

A Truly Healthy Home

Shop vintage

Old garments have had time to release the chemical fabric finishes and volatile compounds that usually come with newer clothing. Natural fabrics are still best, but you may find something older that is a blend of synthetic and natural materials and you just have to buy it because it is one of a kind!

Fix something old or trade with friends

If you come across an old purse, faded jeans, or hand-me-down sweater that seems too nostalgic to throw away or donate, consider having it altered or embellished to make it unique. It's hard to find things that fit perfectly, especially that old pair of worn jeans. Once you do, it's hard to let go, so find ways to mend or improve on your favorites. This is healthy for you, healthy for the environment, and really fun! Have an afternoon gathering where friends exchange clothing and mix and match favorite fabric remnants to patch clothes and create new styles. Provide fashion magazines for inspiration, scissors, and sewing materials. Large sewing needles and yarn can be put to work to adorn ripped hems, while beads and trim can embellish a nice-fitting but plain T-shirt.

Window Coverings

Shedding Light on Synthetic Shades

If you pull the shades before you drop off to sleep, there are some things you should know about traditional window coverings. Any fabric that is "permanent press" such as drapery panels will be treated with toxic formaldehyde. Synthetic draperies, vinyl blinds, and other man-made window coverings are made of materials that off-gas and break down over time, especially when exposed to heat from sunlight or forced-air heating. The gases produced during this process are not only irritating but hormone-disrupting. And yet window coverings are often needed to block out street lights or artificial light to get a good night's sleep. Studies have shown that exposure to light during sleep disrupts production of the hormone melatonin, which is crucial for the immune system. Recent research indicates that the bedroom should be pitch-black. Window coverings can help to block light and, in some cases, decrease noise, another factor for restful sleep.

You can replace synthetic window coverings with woven shades of natural materials or wood blinds (make sure their source is not unsustainable rain-forest logging, a problem with many producers of wooden blinds). You can also have beautiful flat roman shades made from organic cotton or linen. Most shades can be lined to block out all light to give you a restful night's sleep, especially if you are bothered by streetlights, or other exterior light sources. This will help your body's immune system recharge while you sleep.

Air Quality

Good air quality is especially important in the bedroom because we spend long hours breathing deeply while we sleep; our clean air efforts should begin here. A good way to start is to keep pets out of the bedroom—although this will be difficult for those who consider Fido or Fluffy one of the family. The dander, hair, and garden chemicals your pets carry into your home can disrupt your sleep, especially if you have allergies. If it is not possible to keep pets off the bed and out of the bedroom, you should change your bedding, clean, and vacuum more frequently.

Don't forget temperature when you think about air quality. During winter, set the thermostat to 55 degrees or off, health permitting, for bedtime. Experts find that this temperature is ideal for sleeping. In warmer months, increase air movement and ventilation but keep the air-conditioning off unless you're really uncomfortable. Air quality is often better when your heating or air-conditioning is off, unless you have a very efficient air-purification system as a part of your heating and cooling process.

Instant Gratification

Open the windows

If your neighborhood is safe and the air quality outside is pretty good, leave your bedroom windows open. Fresh air can reduce the concentration of chemicals; moving air will help furniture, fabric, and building materials to off-gas more quickly.

Place a plant in your bedroom

Plants are the best natural air filters available. They don't cost much and they really change the atmosphere of your home. Consider plants such as these to add a natural purification device to your decor: areca palm, chrysanthemum, English ivy, peace lily, philodendron, rubber plant, and spider plant. Keep soil fairly dry as wet soil can harbor fungus, molds, or insects. Don't let excess water sit in the drip tray of a houseplant as mold can grow there, too. You can use a soap-based nontoxic spray on the soil of your houseplants to discourage insects.

More Committed?

Make cleaning your bedroom a weekly ritual

Everyone avoids housecleaning sometimes, but if you skip all other rooms or even do a partial cleaning, pay special attention in the bedroom. Dust surfaces, including wood floors, with a damp cotton rag; vacuum carpets with a HEPA filter model. Don't forget to remove spiderwebs in corners, where dust can collect, but if you don't mind one or two spiders, they are part of the ecosystem and help control mosquitoes and flies.

Natural scents

Stop using air fresheners or deodorizers, conventional aerosol room sprays, plug-in fragrance, or any synthetic or chemical fragrance for the air. Use the scents and perfumes of nature to deodorize and create an alluring atmosphere with bowls of leaves and flowers such as lavender buds, beeswax candles with plant-based fragrances, and aromatherapy from essential oils. Be sure that you buy organic lavender rather than any that has been sprayed with pesticides or enhanced with synthetic lavender scent. Most potpourri available in retail stores is some natural material that has been cleaned, colored, scented, and preserved. The chemicals used in this process can be irritating or, at worst, noxious enough to trigger allergy attacks or sensitize individuals.

A Truly Healthy Home

On the floor

Hardwood is the best flooring for a bedroom. If you want a softer feel and look, use natural wool or woven-grass area rugs that can be removed from the room and cleaned regularly.

Children's Rooms

Adult bedrooms can be sanctuaries, retreats, and places for restful slumber, but in the case of a child's bedroom you may have very distinctly different activities happening in one small space. Even in homes with a playroom or area in a family room for toys and craft activities, it is common (especially when little ones first get their own bedroom) for a child's room to hold much more than a crib or bed. Use the main functions of any room as your inspiration for decorating and planning. Mindful of the need for stimulation, play, and storage, you'll want this room to be restful and quiet, safe from drafts and drastic temperature changes.

As you gain awareness of home-building and home-furnishing products and materials, such as off-gassing paint, noxious carpet, toxic bedding, synthetic fabric for clothing, and the potential harm from plastics, you will want to be especially prudent in your child's room. Less is more here—you can always add furniture later when you are sure the wood is free from formaldehyde and toxic finishes. There are many sources for healthy baby furniture, clothing, and toys that you can feel confident about placing in a child's room.

If you're expecting, tell your friends about your concern for a healthy baby room so that they can be aware of the options available when buying gifts and clothing. Create a baby shower registry so friends and family know your preference for non-toxic items.

Because children inevitably put toys into their mouths, knowing what their toys are made of is of utmost importance. Some old toys may contain lead paint or mercury beads enclosed in plastic that can be lethal if ingested. If you buy plastic toys, stay away from toxic polyvinyl chloride (PVC) as much as possible. PVC is commonly used in teethers and soft squeeze toys for young children, beach balls, bath toys, dolls, and other products. Phthalates (the ingredient that makes plastic soft and pliable) have been linked to reproductive and developmental disorders, cancer, and organ damage. Substitute polyethylene or polypropylene, as they are not chlorinated. Toys made from wood with nontoxic paints or finishes are beautiful alternatives to plastics; they are inspiring to make yourself, or you can support woodworking craftspeople.

Don't forget the imagination of a child, developed in quiet playtime before the days of TV, video games, and cell phones. The development of every individual, including intelligence, personality, health, and happiness, begins when that person is a child. The complexities of brain development are far from being understood, but it is clear that the need for natural play is a real one. Set limits on computer, TV, and electronic toy time. Try to make equal time for active exercise outdoors, contemplative nature walks, quiet time reading, coloring, building with construction-type toys, and make-believe. Music and art are inspiring; many companies sell sustainably made instruments such as drums and nontoxic craft materials. Toys and games in nontoxic materials that focus on teamwork and collaboration teach cooperation. The formative years can set patterns that lead to a healthier, more balanced adult life.

Instant Gratification

Toy box

Create or purchase storage bins or drawers to hold toys, because some chemicals and finishes on toys can be kept at bay when contained. This also creates good habits and helps to eliminate clutter in a child's room. An orderly house is easier to keep clean and free of dust and dirt, plus it is so nice for you and your children to be able to find things when you want them!

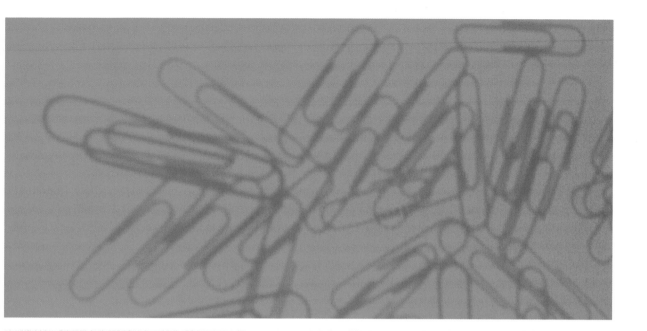

CHAPTER 4

Work & Play

Entertainment rooms, home offices, and space for art, crafts, and projects are not altogether new but the technology and toxic materials that have made their way into our homes create new challenges.

Multitasking spaces often look and feel chaotic, overloaded with furniture, objects, and supplies that need to be accessed easily. If your family has a bill-paying center, computer, TV, or a table used for homework, work, and crafts, you will need to consider logistics when you improve the health of these rooms. Simple issues that you will confront may be the importance of tidiness and respect for face-to-face interaction in the midst of home technology.

Healthy and efficient work spaces are often enclosed or separate from common areas and should enjoy natural light. The furniture must be comfortable and ergonomic and work surfaces accommodating. You can decrease stress from clutter and visual chaos with a consistency of colors and materials as well as efficient, well-designed closed-storage systems. Closed storage may help protect you from chemical off-gassing from office and craft supplies and limit exposure to undesirable electrical fields.

As issues of placement can have an impact on the function and emotional satisfaction of any living space, the entertainment room, home office, and craft studio should be well planned. It is important to be able to work without having your back to the door, and it is crucial to create a serene workplace.

Televisions, computers, and other office equipment contain hazardous materials. These include lead, cadmium, and mercury, all highly toxic heavy metals. Health effects of lead and mercury include permanent brain damage, reproductive and developmental problems, and possibly cancer. Cadmium is a known carcinogen that can also cause kidney and liver damage. The plastic housings and circuit boards in computers and some office machinery are made with brominated flame retardants. These contaminants are suspected endocrine disrupters and have been shown to interrupt brain development and perhaps cause cancer; they have been discovered at increasing levels in humans and fish. While the greatest threat from many technology toxins is to workers manufacturing the systems (and the environment surrounding the factory), there is some evidence that exposure to certain chemicals can occur during computer use.

TVs, Computers, EMFs

Waves of energy radiate out all around us every day from power lines, television transmitters, cell phone towers, and other large sources. Our own neural pathways use electrical impulses to send information from the brain throughout the human body. Every home supplied with electricity has an elevated level of electromagnetic fields (EMFs). Metal objects magnify these electrical fields. The danger of the interaction of these energy waves with the normal level of electrical current in our bodies is under scrutiny. The electromagnetic processes occurring in our bodies account for much of the self-regulating mechanisms, including hormone management and immune-system function. In several documented cases individuals have reacted in devastating ways to common household EMF levels. In some instances where individuals could not determine the source of allergic reactions, headaches, skin reactions, and general malaise, lowering EMF exposure improved symptoms.

While electricity and electrical appliances exist in every area of your home, the TV room and home office are subjected to major sources of increased EMFs. Besides the television, computers, and computer monitors, other sources include printers, copy machines, faxes, and any "black box" plug such as those found on cell phone chargers.

Instant Gratification

Get a safe distance from the TV

If you have purchased a gauss meter, you can determine at exactly what distance the level of EMFs drops off significantly. If you need to use a basic rule of thumb, two to six feet is a good start. Children should not sit on the floor in front of the television if possible, especially on carpet, as the synthetics in most carpets create an electrostatic charge.

Surge protectors

Turn off the switch on surge protectors when not in use. Better yet, unplug the surge protector from the wall socket. You can also have an outlet wired by an electrician to connect to a wall switch so that when you leave the computer area, turning off the wall switch shuts off current to that outlet and any surge protector or items plugged into that outlet. (Put a sign on this wall switch that says, "Don't turn this off if I'm working!" to prevent lost data.) Know that just because a device is "off" doesn't mean that it no longer emits a powerful EMF.

Lower computer EMFs

You can buy EMF shields for most computer screens. Most laptop screens have lower EMF readings than desktop models. Standby mode still creates a higher EMF level than if the computer is completely powered down. Remember to turn off the power to your printer or any machine that doesn't need to be in standby mode. Many new multitasking combo devices go into power-save mode if not used for a while, but power up if a fax is received or a document is sent to the printer. After you power down your computer, remember to turn off its power supply either by unplugging it or turning off a switch wired to that outlet.

More Committed?

Limit time spent watching TV and using the computer

Time seems to float away while your gaze is on the TV or computer screen. Keep a clock or kitchen timer nearby, take breaks, and move around. Studies show decreased brain-wave activity in individuals while watching TV. It has even been seen that brain waves are actually less active while watching TV than while doing nothing! Set TV-free nights or time limits on TV watching and computer use. Make time for family games or a walk after dinner (which helps digestion and improves quality of sleep).

Keep them separate

Separate your work space from sleeping area and family room if it isn't already. If possible, designate a separate room with a door that closes for the home office.

Buy an armoire or a cabinet to house the TV or computer

There are several ways to enclose these devices that can help to decrease your exposure to EMFs. The added benefit to placing technology in a closed cabinet is that it helps to decrease dust and clutter and can create a more serene and polished look for a room where you need to multitask. Several companies sell mini home office stations with pull-out keyboard trays, "pocket doors" (that completely slide into the cabinet), and shelves designed to hold printers, faxes, and supplies.

Buy a multitasking machine

Many of the new multi purpose office machines are more energy efficient than older models. These units also use one ink cartridge, saving you from buying chemicals for several different machines. Often these units are equipped with power-save modes that usually emit lower EMFs.

A Truly Healthy Home

Awareness

Make it a family project to understand EMFs. Take the time to test every room in your home and look for ways to change your habits. Set an example by turning off lights and unplugging household appliances when not in use.

Redesign the entertainment center and computer cabinet

Having a custom entertainment system or work station built for you by a contractor, carpenter, or craftsperson can be costly but it will give you more functional floor space for other activities and can create a very seamless and tidy look for a room of many uses. Especially if your work space is connected to your living room or kitchen, you'll want ways to limit visual clutter and keep technology enclosed and shielded. Make sure your carpenter understands how to use healthy wood finishes and will be willing to use non-formaldehyde plywood or fiberboard if choosing nonsolid wood components for the boxes. Function and design are of utmost importance in a custom-built unit; you can select many specialized hardware pieces that maximize space and versatility. You want this piece to be durable and high quality. The design should appeal to your sense of style and be integrated with your home's architectural features.

Office Supplies

Bleached paper, ink cartridges, batteries, pens, glues, and a multitude of other office supplies are made from chemicals that present health dangers. Bleached white office paper, besides usually coming from tree pulp from forests, is processed with chlorine, releasing extremely toxic dioxin into the environment. Office papers are also treated with other chemicals for various functions and finishes.

The best thing you can do for yourself and the planet in terms of paper is to buy chlorine-free, tree-free recycled papers with high postconsumer waste content (such as 90 percent), so that the "recycled" content is not pulp from sawdust from the floor of sawmills. Tree-free means made from plant materials such as kenaf or hemp instead of forests; some labels say "no virgin wood fibers are used."

Look for nontoxic pens and other safer supplies for your work space—a good art supply store is often a source for labeled nontoxic materials that can be put to use in the home office. For essential materials that still pose health risks, take measures to reduce exposure, including good ventilation, secure closed storage, and sparing use. You can reduce danger of spills by keeping the work space well organized. De-clutter your desk (and reduce dust) with unique storage bins from natural materials.

Reduce Your Junk Mail

Not only does junk mail waste paper and expose your household to chemical dyes and coated papers, but it is a time and space waster. If you ever worry that an important bill might fall between the pages of an unsolicited flyer or glossy catalog and hate taking the time to sift through the irritations to find what you want, you can take steps to reduce junk mail. Online services can help you do this, but some types of mass mail are hard to stop. Anytime you send out correspondence or order something, write on the paperwork that you do not want your information sold. Some first class mail can be marked "refused, return to sender" and placed in the outgoing mail. Use the self-stamped return envelope or postcard of a company or organization to mail your message that you want to be taken out of their database. Recycle what you continue to get and start using online services to pay bills and transact purchases if this is comfortable for you. It will decrease the chlorine, chemicals, inks, and coatings that come into your home on the paper from your mail.

Proper Recycling or Disposal of Toxic Supplies

Ineffective recycling practices put people at risk. Batteries and used ink-cartridges that are dropped into the wastebasket can release potentially harmful ingredients into your home and ultimately into the environment. You can recycle these items; you may, however, want to know what happens once you drop these items off. The vast majority of technology waste that is collected for recycling in industrialized nations gets shipped to other countries for processing. The result is that poor communities bear the environmental brunt for processing obsolete electronics, especially from toxins leaching into their water supplies. You can minimize your impact in this as in other activities by efforts to not be wasteful, and looking for less toxic alternatives. Look into how to safely recycle old cell phones, computers, and other office equipment, or donate them to a nonprofit.

Rechargeable batteries are a partial solution. Your health will be improved by keeping used cartridges and other problem items in an enclosed recycling container until pick-up day or until you have enough items to warrant a trip to the recycling center. Don't leave spent batteries outside in the rain in open recycle containers. Be sure to keep different types of items separate from each other according to the requirements of your recycling service. Keep office-related recyclables separate from the usual cans, bottles, and newspapers.

Instant Gratification

Make a system

Create a safe and unique battery and ink-cartridge recycling system. Consider unusual containers that close securely to store paper or to hold toxic recyclables.

More Committed?

Create your own stationery

Create notepads for phone messages and lists from brown paper bags, unbleached and untreated paper, and recycled paper from your own office waste. Have fun mixing and matching different paper types and colors and use a simple binding that is decorative and sturdy. You can buy a leather needle and hole puncher to create your own stitched bindings with natural cord or string.

Ergonomic Furniture

Body mechanics involve the interrelationship between parts of the body during movement and at rest. Injurious body mechanics can develop for many reasons. Ergonomics relate to the study of correct body positions for optimal comfort and function. This has been applied to the design of many objects to make them more comfortable, safer, and easier to use.

Ergonomic specialists and physical therapists help people remedy chronic conditions such as hand, arm, neck, and back pain that have developed from overuse and poor posture. Trauma from accidents and repetitive stress injuries such as carpal tunnel syndrome can be helped with an understanding of ergonomics. Repetitive strain injuries are often helped with better posture and regular breaks from the offending activity.

Take the time to look into your furniture design and layout and you can probably cure some basic problems by finding positions that feel most comfortable and natural. For instance, your computer screen should be positioned so that your head and neck are not strained when you work. Get help from others to actively observe everyone in the family using a work station and sitting in their favorite TV-watching or reading chair. Notice when you feel unsupported, uncomfortable, and strained and help others to observe their own body positions. You may have perfectly functional furniture that needs to be adjusted or repositioned, or you may need merely to change some personal habits. If necessary, replace essential furniture with ergonomically correct, properly sized pieces made from materials such as non-formaldehyde particleboard or sustainably harvested wood.

Ergonomically correct chairs are much more effective if they are set up in conjunction with proper distance from tabletops, computer keyboards, and screens. Well-designed furniture and proper placement can be undermined by bad posture habits and long periods of inactivity or repetitive actions. Take a look at your posture and the way you interact with objects you use or furniture you sit on. Ask a physical therapist, exercise or dance instructor, chiropractor, or your family physician to show you how to improve your posture. Learn about how your sitting habits may create chronic conditions. You can apply this information to a redesign of your home workplace.

Instant Gratification

Take a break and stretch

Get up every hour or two, walk around the block, or at least change your position and stop what you are doing. Stretch your body by standing and reaching to the ceiling and then take a moment to feel for areas that are tight. Focus a moment on those tight or sore spots by carefully massaging the area with your hand or stretching the muscle.

Practice healthy sitting

Try this sitting exercise on the floor to get a sense of how it feels to sit in a healthy, ergonomic position.

1. Concentrate on keeping your spine straight and your "sitz bones" (the bones you feel when you are seated) in contact with the floor.

2. Keep your shoulder blades down and pulled together on the back. Then lift your shoulders high, pull them back, and pull them down. This should feel like you are sliding your shoulder blades down your spine and squeezing the space in between them.

3. Relax your neck and head. Most people have a tendency to stick their head forward and down after a long day or while driving. Open your mouth slightly to relax your jaw and imagine that a string or cord is attached to the top of your head. Visualize this cord pulling your head and neck upward with a steady and gentle motion.

More Committed?

Research different options for seating

There are many ways to sit and work comfortably. It's a matter of personal preference and body type and structure. Take a field trip to an office furniture store to assess kneeling chairs, "active" stools, and even a large exercise ball. A kneeling chair puts your body in a position that allows weight to distribute more evenly throughout your lower body and puts less strain on the lower back. The "active" stool or a large exercise ball (made from natural rubber or latex, not petrochemicals) can help deal with chronic discomfort due to inactivity or bad posture because it demands an active way to sit. Active sitting works to combat bad posture habits because it makes you more aware of your body and keeps muscles working while you do activities that typically keep you inactive.

Lighting

Lighting is one of the most magical mediums to change the mood of a room and can easily be used to create a healthier home environment. Re-creating a living environment that more closely resembles a balanced exposure to daylight and sunlight with restful periods in complete darkness can reconnect us to natural rhythms. In rooms where we spend creative or working time and rely on our eyesight to make our accomplishments possible, good and healthy sources of light are essential.

A lack of natural light can be detrimental to our health, affecting mineral absorption and function of the endocrine system, as well as creating problems such as vitamin deficiency and depression or Seasonal Affective Disorder (SAD). SAD is common in winter but similar emotional effects happen with too much time spent in other low-light daytime conditions. Overexposure to fluorescents and other artificial light can also be harmful, contributing to vision problems as well as mood disorders, anxiety, or depression.

There are many ways to enhance the quality of light in your home. For the home office, limiting the use of artificial light—including incandescent but especially fluorescent and halogen lights—can make a big difference in the feel and health of this room. (The high level of EMFs and sometimes off-gassing of toxins from older fluorescents are also of concern.)

Full-Spectrum Light Bulbs

In the home office, art studio, or anywhere you work, read, or sit for extended periods of time, full-spectrum light bulbs can be a simple but dramatic change for healthy quality of light. These light bulbs simulate the spectrum of light found in natural daylight and are much better for your eyes, sense of well-being, and overall health than other types of artificial light. They are also designed to last longer than standard bulbs, so they are cost-effective and create less waste.

Natural Light

Natural light is incomparable for health over other sources, but bright sunshine can strain or damage the eyes, as well as cause excessive heat and damage to materials, art, furniture, and flooring. It's best to situate your work areas so that you are exposed to and can work by natural light, but be careful of glare as the sun makes its course outside your windows.

Keep light-sensitive supplies as well as photographs and artwork safe. Anywhere in the house, try to keep upholstery or other fabrics that are particularly light sensitive out of direct sunlight or cover them with a light-colored sheet or throw during bright sunny days.

Skylights and high, clerestory windows expose a room to natural daylight that is fairly evenly distributed. These light sources diminish glare and, if insulated, can be energy efficient and prevent heat loss or overheating.

Art & Hobby Materials

Making space at home for creative pursuits helps you and your family cultivate your talents and gifts. Although having a space for art at home is more convenient than an art studio somewhere away from your house, proximity will present some health risks from the use and storage of materials.

Pigments, Solvents, and Other Dangers

Legal standards exist to label and control toxic ingredients in art and hobby materials, but exposure remains a health risk, involving the possibility of cancer, nervous system damage, lung damage, or skin reactions. Dangerous materials include chlorinated hydrocarbons (solvents) in ink, varnish, paint removers, rubber cement, and aerosol sprays; petroleum distillates (solvents) in paint and rubber cement thinners, spray adhesives, silk-screen inks, and glycol ethers; and acetates in photography products, lacquer thinners, paints, and aerosol sprays.

Other toxic ingredients include lead in ceramic glazes, stained-glass materials, and many pigments; cadmium in silver solders, pigments, ceramic glazes, and fluxes; chromium in paint pigments and ceramic colors; manganese dioxide in ceramic colors and some oil and acrylic paints; cobalt pigments in some blue oils and acrylics; formaldehyde as a preservative in many acrylic paints and photographic products; and aromatic hydrocarbons in paint and varnish removers, aerosol sprays, and permanent markers.

Clays and Enamels

Colorful polymer craft clays feel like natural clay and stay soft at room temperature but can be easily hardened in a kitchen oven instead of a high-temperature kiln. Those desirable qualities come from the undesirable, carcinogenic ingredient PVC, containing significant levels of phthalates. Even after washing, phthalate residues can remain on the hands. When baking, phthalates can be released into the air, raising the risk of inhalation exposure.

Enamels are usually lead-based and can contain other toxic metals such as cadmium and nickel. Use lead-free enamels whenever possible, and make sure kilns are vented outside.

In pottery as well, outside vented kilns are important, as is a careful choice of materials—most potters know to avoid lead glazes and lead frits, but many don't know that flint, feldspars, fluorspar, and compounds containing barium, lithium, manganese, or nickel can also be toxic. Children should work only in a pottery studio where materials are consistently nontoxic, as they are more highly susceptible to the toxins and dusts than are adults.

Choose Nontoxic Products

Let awareness guide you in your choice of what art or craft medium you'd like to pursue, and look for nontoxic choices when buying supplies. In painting and print-making, ready-mixed water-based paints or inks can be used.

Choose art supplies that are certified by the Art & Creative Materials Institute (ACMI) — a helpful guideline, although its logos and ratings are not a guarantee of safety. Don't rely solely on ACMI logos for help in choosing safer products for children.

Because some techniques require certain materials with no safe alternative, minimizing exposure may be the best you can do when you are committed to a particular medium. If you must be exposed to paint dust or dry pigments, use an adequate level of respirator, and follow safety procedures for cleanup.

Instant Gratification

Open the windows or work outside

Ventilate your working space thoroughly whenever using solvents or other chemicals, such as in painting or print-making. If your project is portable, set a worktable out under a shady tree.

More Committed?

Try digital photography

Photography presents a number of toxic hazards that are difficult to avoid. Minimize exposure to photo chemicals by using gloves and mixing chemicals in a mixing box with holes in the sides for gloved hands, and provide adequate ventilation. Children under twelve should avoid the darkroom.

The creative potential of digital photography and picture editing offers an alternative, as does the idea of collage work recycling extra prints. The latter can be inked, painted over, and otherwise embellished to give unwanted prints a creative fate other than going to the landfill.

A Truly Healthy Home

An indoor/outdoor art studio

Convert a screened porch or construct a latticed gazebo dedicated to creative activities. Consider a picnic table and benches to hold sprawling art projects and use old glass jars and metal cans to store art supplies. Create a storage system for kids' craft projects.

Bathrooms

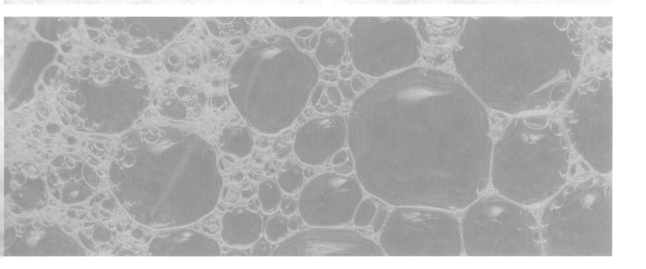

A healthy bathroom can serve as your personal spa to retreat to for long soaks in a tub of therapeutic water, surrounded by an inviting atmosphere created by natural materials and candlelight.

Sounds inviting, doesn't it? But before you spend hours soaking in the delights of a pampering bathroom, you want to make sure it's a healthy place to be relaxing in. In that regard, the bathroom offers its own special challenges.

With high moisture content in a usually small space, bathrooms are particularly prone to harboring germs and dangerous mold. Adding insult to injury, many of the products that make us feel our best—fragrant silky moisturizers, cleansers, and soaps—can actually be doing us the most harm. Even your choice of towels and shower curtains can affect your family's health. And water quality, frequently impaired by harsh chemicals, can do its own share of harm. So how do you make your bathroom clean, pampering, and, above all, safe?

Ventilation & Light

Bathrooms need extra ventilation due to humidity and often lack natural light due to small or absent windows. Open the bathroom window anytime you can to discourage moist or stagnant air. These conditions can lead to the growth of harmful molds, which have been shown to increase allergies and worsen asthma symptoms in many people. Removing molds and moisture from your bathroom is one of the best ways to go from harmful to healthy!

If privacy is a concern, consider a sheer linen or cotton gauze curtain that lets light and air in but keeps prying eyes out. Just be sure to wash the curtain regularly along with your bathroom towels and rugs. A curtain with button or snap fasteners is ideal for frequent washing.

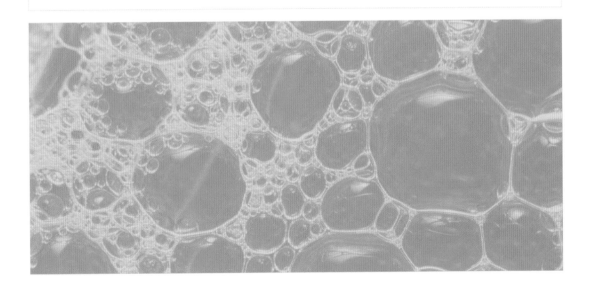

Instant Gratification

Nontoxic cleaning

Clean your bathroom thoroughly using only nontoxic cleaning products. In this confined and often unventilated space, mold remedies, such as chlorine bleach, can produce such noxious fumes that the cure is often worse than the complaint. See the section on safe cleaning products at the back of the book for alternatives that are healthier for you and less polluting when you send them down the drain. Keep toxic cleaning products in a storage area with other household cleaning products until you can use them up or safely dispose of them.

More Committed?

Vents, screens, and seals

Install vents and screen your bathroom windows to allow you to keep them open while showering or bathing and for at least twenty to thirty minutes after you leave the bathroom to be sure all excess moisture has had enough time to escape. Remove old bathtub caulk and replace with a new, nontoxic caulk product. Poorly sealed bathtubs are one of the first pathways for mold to grow. One way to ensure that you get a good seal is to make sure your tub area is very dry and clean before you recaulk the seam between tub and tile. (A trick to get the gap well filled is to fill the tub with water just before caulking, but be sure the joint is very dry. Because the weight of the water expands the joint, you can drain the tub once the caulk is cured and it will have created a very nice full bead.)

A Truly Healthy Home

Ventilation

Replace bathroom windows that don't open. Install a motorized ventilation fan in the ceiling of the bathroom and let it run during and after your bath or shower—helpful if opening the window makes the room too cold. Install a skylight or Solatube for better natural light.

Radiant heat

Install radiant heat in your floors when you update the flooring to eliminate the need for an electric or forced-air heating system. Ideally, all the floors in your home could have radiant heat, but a bathroom update is an easy way to start.

Personal Care Products & Cosmetics

Let's face it, personal care products are fun. They come in pretty packages, smell nice, and tempt us with all sorts of extravagant promises: smoother skin or shinier, thicker hair. So who can blame us if we get a little carried away? Many consumers average the use of twenty-five personal care products a day, exposing skin to over two hundred chemicals. Be aware that most of the shampoos, hair gels, cleansers, skin creams, cosmetics, and other personal care products we love so much contain harmful elements that irritate the skin. At their worst they can cause nerve damage or cancer or disrupt the immune system.

The cosmetic industry is underregulated and therefore free to use multiple chemicals to scent, preserve, or bind preparations. Some have been proven to be quite toxic and dangerous, especially to children and anyone else with sensitive immune systems. You should avoid as many of these chemicals as possible. But don't despair. A multitude of pure and natural products is available in your health food store, online and through local distributors. These not only improve your health, but they are often of higher quality, nicer smelling, and less expensive than many other conventional personal care products.

Your skin is the largest organ of your body. It serves to protect you as well as to release accumulated toxins. Your skin breathes, regulating your body and allowing the release of heat while allowing many things in. When you apply a skin-care product to the surface of your skin, it is absorbed into your body. Given that in the course of a day you expose yourself to many products that sit on your skin for hours and enter your bloodstream, doesn't it make sense to choose these as carefully as you choose the food you eat?

Inventory Your Personal Care Products

To get started, set aside an hour or so to take out all of the skin products, shampoos, lotions, and styling products that live in your cabinets, in the shower stall, or in the medicine cabinet. Inventory everything—yes, that means all those old products in pretty packages that you don't use, as well as everything you use on a daily basis. Be relentless. Encourage other family members to join in.

Review the checklist in this chapter against the list of contents on the labels of the products you use. If any of the substances on the list of things to avoid appears among the first five ingredients, you know that these products contain a high measure of harmful ingredients. Decide what to do with the products that are high in toxicity. Use them up and vow never to buy them again. Or take a stand and toss them right away. Open the containers of the items you feel you must keep and smell: does it smell off or rancid? Throw it out.

The more you can substitute synthetic products with ones made of safer plant-based ingredients, the healthier you will be. One problem with petroleum by-products is that they are connected with some form of human carcinogen either by themselves or as they break down or combine with other chemicals. There are many plant-derived natural sudsing agents from materials such as coconut that do not strip your skin or expose you or your child's skin to petrochemical ingredients. Portable hand sanitizers are commonly used for convenience, but nothing beats hand washing with pure soap and water to ward off germs. Simple alcohol-based sanitizers are fine to use in a pinch, but soaps containing antibacterial or antimicrobial ingredients such as triclosan may contribute to the rise of drug-resistant bacteria.

Remember the Children

Not everyone shows sensitivity to many potentially harmful ingredients, but be aware that their manufacture is harmful to the environment. Consider the well-being of your children, too—kids are using cosmetics, deodorants, and fragrances at younger and younger ages. They may not appreciate your interference now, but helping them to swap to healthy products when they're young may save them lots of sick days in the future.

What to Avoid and What to Look For in Personal Care Products

Cosmetic companies sugarcoat potentially harmful ingredients with labeling such as "dermatologist tested," "noncomedogenic," "hypoallergenic," "designed for sensitive skin," "laboratory tested," and "our research shows." Since the companies that sell the ingredients do most of the research, the majority of claims are less than helpful. This list of ingredients to avoid will steer you in the right direction, regardless of marketing promises. These definitions are based on scientific studies and reports; new information is being discovered all the time, so take this list as a starting place and make a point to be informed.

Avoid the following common toxins in personal care products

Aerosol propellants (used to dispense a product more quickly) contribute to poor air quality, respiratory problems.

Aluminum by-products (color in cosmetics and anti-wetness agent in antiperspirants and deodorants) are carcinogenic, toxic, and mutagenic.

Benzoates (preservatives) are found in many forms in multiple products, can cause adverse reactions, are toxic, carcinogenic, and mutagenic.

Coal tar "colors" (coloring agents such as FD&C Blue 1, Green 3, Yellow 5&6; D&C Red 33) cause severe allergic reactions, asthma attacks, fatigue, nervousness, headaches, nausea, lack of concentration and are carcinogenic.

Diethanolamine (DEA, TEA) (synthetic solvent, detergent, and humectant found in hair dyes, lotions, creams, bubble baths, liquid dishwasher detergents, and laundry soaps) can be harmful for the liver, kidneys, and pancreas and may cause cancer in various organs. It has also been known to irritate skin, eyes, and mucous membranes. It poses health risks especially to infants and young children. It forms nitrosamines known to be carcinogens and causes allergic reactions and contact dermatitis.

DMDM hydantoin or MDM (formaldehyde), trade name: Formalin (used in nail polishes and hardeners, soaps, cosmetics, and hair-growing products), colorless gas with vapors that are very toxic when inhaled; extremely irritating to mucous membranes; ingestion can produce severe abdominal pain, internal bleeding, vertigo, a loss of ability to urinate, and coma; a severe skin irritant and a suspected carcinogen. Its use in cosmetics is banned in Japan and Sweden.

Fragrance (containing phthalates used to mask chemical smells and create product identity and allure) can cause allergic reactions and irritation in many individuals.

Fluoride (used to strengthen teeth), linked by researchers to cancer, dental deformity, arthritis, allergic reactions, and Crohn's disease; fluoridated toothpaste is especially dangerous to young children, who tend to swallow it after brushing their teeth; a toxic manufacturing by-product.

Glycol, a chemical used in products such as antifreeze; used in cosmetics as a humectant—emulsifier and moisturizer—derived from animal or vegetable, natural or synthetic sources; glycerin substitute. The FDA cautions manufacturers that glycols may cause adverse reactions in users. They have been shown to be carcinogenic, mutagenic, and toxic. Propylene glycol (used to break down proteins and in deodorants) has

caused liver abnormalities and kidney damage in laboratory animals. Diethylene glycol and carbitol are considered toxic. Ethylene glycol is a suspected bladder carcinogen.

Isopropyl alchohol (solvent used to change other ingredient qualities) may cause headaches, dizziness, depression, nausea, and vomiting.

Methyl, propyl, butyl, and ethyl parabens (the most common preservatives and antibacterials used in a variety of personal care products, especially creams and lotions), petroleum-based; can cause dermatitis and allergic reactions and can be hormone disruptors.

Nitrates, nitrosamines, and sulfur compounds (in shampoos), nitrosamines can form in all cosmetic ingredients containing amines and amino derivatives with nitrogen compounds. Nitrosamines are known carcinogens. Studies have shown that additives react with the ingredients of food supplements or cosmetics to form carcinogenic nitrates and dioxin, which may enter the circulatory system with each shampoo or each oral ingestion. The end result is that these harmful substances can be retained in the liver, heart, eyes, kidneys, and muscles for several years.

Petrolatum or mineral oil (used to hold in moisture) disrupts the body's ability to release toxins via the skin; promotes acne; leads to dryness and premature aging.

Phthalates are known to be toxic or carcinogenic or to cause problems with fertility (many types of plastic packaging are made flexible by adding phthalates that may leach from the plastic).

Quaternium 15 (formaldehyde) (used in various industries as a preservative; formaldehyde-releasing agents are found in skin, body, and hair-care products, antiperspirants, nail polish) irritates the respiratory system; may cause skin reactions, heart palpitations, joint pain, allergies, depression, headaches, chronic fatigue, weakens the immune system in some individuals.

Sodium lauryl sulfate (SLS) (a surfactant—creates suds, breaks down other ingredients; an ingredient in 90 percent of commercially available shampoo and conditioners; found in toothpaste, cream, lotions, car-wash soap, engine degreaser, and garage-floor cleaners) corrodes hair follicles, impedes hair growth, and can penetrate the eyes, brain, and liver and remain there for a long time. It can also degenerate cell membranes, change genetic information (mutagenic) in cells, and damage the immune system. It is further reported to cause eye irritations, skin rashes, hair loss, dandruff, and allergic reactions. It may also lead to blindness or cataracts.

Toluene (obtained from petroleum; used as a solvent in cosmetics, especially nail polishes and dyes; it is also found in pharmaceuticals and gasoline as a blending agent) resembles benzene; if ingested may cause mild anemia and liver damage, and may irritate the skin and respiratory tract.

Triclosan (antibacterial) can lead to resistant strains of germs.

Healthy Ingredient Substitutes:

- **Astringents and aftershaves:** witch hazel or other herbs that act as astringents (such as tea tree or melaleuca oil) and antibacterials

- **Deodorants:** baking soda, white clay, deodorant crystals

- **Perfumes:** essential oils that provide nontoxic fragrances to scent shampoo, bath soaks, or even, in the case of peppermint, to flavor toothpaste

- **Soaps and cleansing agents:** castile soap, coconut oil, and olive oil-based soap

- **Toothpastes:** baking soda, salt, mint and other essential oils

Switch from Perfume to Essential Oils

Because scent is such a strong and primitive sense, we might use scented products or perfumes that evoke irresistible positive memories or emotional attachments. By all means indulge in the world's good smells, but consider that synthetic fragrance is one of the most common allergens (for the wearer or for nearby sufferers) and one of the first ingredients in many products. It makes sense to buy the purest form of natural fragrance available: essential oils. You can create a new palette of scents to indulge in and quite possibly new memories to go along with them!

Use essential oils in place of perfumes, to scent liquid soap, blend with lotion, or to create an aromatherapy bath designed for your needs—to relax and calm worn nerves, invigorate and enliven your senses, or soothe sore muscles. Many companies offer blends for specific ailments or desired effects such as stress relief.

Some important things to keep in mind about buying essential oils: buy organic, responsibly wild-crafted essential oils when possible. Some oils are distilled with chemicals and others are blended with "carrier" oils to extend the use to massage oils, body rubs, or lighter facial oils. It's best to buy the purest essential oils you can from a reputable source and educate yourself about the best uses of each type. Have fun mixing and experimenting with new oils and build a library to suit your mood.

Some common essential oils most conducive to good health include:

- **Citrus** soothes psyche, calms, energizes while relieving nervous tension

- **Lavender** induces sleep, alleviates stress, reduces depression and nervous tension

- **Lemongrass** helps sedate the nervous system, soothes headaches, stimulates the thyroid

- **Peppermint** clears nasal passages (do not apply peppermint oil directly to the skin)

- **Pine** is an antiseptic for the respiratory tract, soothes mental stress, and relieves anxiety

- **Rosemary** encourages intuition and enhances memory

- **Sage** is for cleansing and detoxification, remedies mental strain and exhaustion

Purchase Only Chlorine-Free Paper Products

Switch to chlorine-free, dioxin-free toilet paper, cosmetic pads, and feminine products. Conventional products often contain chlorine-bleached paper or fiber. Whether highly chlorinated wood pulp (rayon) or low-grade cotton treated with pesticides, you and the environment are exposed to ongoing doses of toxins in the manufacture, use, and disposal of such products. The world is waiting for safe alternatives to become the norm—in the meantime, your local health food store carries chlorine-free paper and feminine products.

Switch to Fluoride-Free, Natural Toothpaste

Flossing, brushing regularly, and using a natural, alcohol-free mouthwash are great ways to help your mouth, teeth, and gums stay healthy and cavity-free without fluoride. Get regular cleanings at your dentist's and teach good hygiene habits to your children early on. Limiting sweets and drinking lots of water can help to reduce plaque buildup. Tongue-cleaning tools (an old tradition in India) can decrease the amount of bacteria in the mouth and help sweeten the breath. Fluoride does help to decrease cavities, but potential side effects of this chemical seem a high price to pay. Read up on the latest studies on fluoride to make your own decision.

Instant Gratification

Change your lipstick or lip balm

One of the easiest healthy changes is to kiss your petroleum-based lipstick or lip balm goodbye. Many lipsticks and lip balms have mentholatum or other fragrance and flavor added to mask the chemicals, but over time (and especially if you have kept a lipstick or lip balm for too long) the underlying ingredients begin to break down, go bad, or become more noticeable than the ingredient used to mask them. Natural lip products, such as those derived from beeswax or plant oils actually nourish your lips and keep them softer and more attractive, decreasing your needs for the product.

Stop wearing nail polish, or at least take a break

Stop getting acrylic nails in a nail salon or painting your nails at home. The fumes are bad for your health and bad for the Earth's atmosphere. Keep your kids away from regular nail polish, too. Have fun smooshing up blueberries or strawberries into a colorful natural dye they can use instead.

Move your medicines

Steam is not good for medicines. Move them to a closet away from the bathroom and of course out of children's reach. Discard outdated medicines and prescriptions by taking them to a pharmacy for safe disposal: *do not flush them away* or throw them in the garbage (these substances are toxic to other creatures in the environment).

Natural healing

Look for alternative health-care remedies for colds and flu under the guidance of your physician or a reputable health-care practitioner. Alternative remedies can be found at your local health food store, but do more research than just reading the labels—herbal substances can be just as powerful as prescription drugs.

Fight germs

Replace your toothbrush on a frequent basis as well as items such as mascara that come into contact with your eyes, nose, or mouth. Wash your towels frequently and sun dry them if you can. Wash your hands throughout the day and take good care of yourself to prevent catching a cold or the flu.

Bath salts

Health food stores carry natural sea salt that makes for a great soak: sprinkle the salt and a few drops of your favorite essential oil into the bath just before stepping in. You can keep sea salt infused with essential oil fragrances in an ornamental glass jar or bottle with a cork stopper—this makes a great Healthy Home gift once labeled and tied with a ribbon or string.

More Committed?

Go natural

Stop dying your hair, or switch to a more natural process or product. The conventional coloring process is accomplished with the use of very powerful chemicals. If you color your hair at home, look to the health food store for more natural alternatives, but do read the ingredient labels. Ammonia-free hair color is a good place to start. Switching to less harsh products means, over time, that your hair will be healthier and more vibrant without artificial color. You can use some household products to create shine: vinegar and lemon for blondes and dark, strong coffee as a rinse to richen brunette shades.

Sweat it out

Switch to a natural deodorant on days when your activity level is lower. You may not want to share your experiments in the world of natural deodorants with others, but do pay attention to how you smell when you are particularly healthy and fit. If you sweat a lot, drink plenty of water and shower after working out: your body is releasing toxins. If you do use traditional deodorant, opt for a non-antiperspirant brand to let your body release toxins, or at least use antiperspirants minimally. The healthier you are, the less you will need topical odor prevention.

A Truly Healthy Home

Old-time treatments

Take a trip back in time: use ingredients that you have in the kitchen or pantry to cleanse, moisturize, and pamper yourself the old-fashioned way. Milk (you can use powdered) can be a luxurious addition to the bath to make skin smooth and silky. The enzymes in fruit and the acid in dairy products such as yogurt make great exfoliants. Many of the oils that you find in fine natural personal care products can be purchased at your health food store and used directly on the skin and hair, such as apricot kernel oil, sesame oil, safflower oil (for light moisturizing), coconut oil, jojoba oil, and olive oil (for dry skin or hair). If your skin is irritated, a lukewarm oatmeal bath works wonders: add ground whole organic oats to your bath and rinse off in cool water. Try a little egg yolk rubbed onto your face to tighten pores and make your skin supersoft.

Replace all your personal care products and cosmetics with nontoxic alternatives

This could take time and some getting used to because many personal care products become part of our ritual and identity. We become attached to a particular scent, or find products we like and become devoted to them. But making the switch to nontoxic products will open up a new world of companies that use high-quality ingredients in wonderfully scented organic, pure, or natural products. Many of these products are less expensive than conventional items and work better! How to identify these products? Learn a few prefixes and suffixes that indicate toxic products from the list on page 118-20, or bring a copy of it with you to the store. Keep in mind that products can include one organic ingredient or several natural additions and yet still be loaded with petrochemicals and synthetic fragrance. Read labels carefully, then have fun trying the items you find that pass the test!

Water Filtration, Chlorine 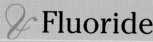 Fluoride

We all love a long soak in the bathtub or a steaming hot shower. What we might not like nearly as much, however, is what's actually in our water. Public water supplies are treated to kill bacteria and viruses. Chlorine is the most common chemical used to treat public water sources. We're told that the chemicals used to treat our water are safe when used in the approved concentrations allowed by public drinking water standards and that the methods of water treatment pose no danger to our health.

Most of the chemicals used in water treatment break down into compounds known to cause immune-system dysfunction and nerve-system disruption. The problem is that very little study has been done to evaluate the cumulative effects of these compounds, especially for children or other people whose immune systems are still developing or have been sensitized.

Chlorine kills bacteria, but you might wonder whether it makes sense to drink, bathe in, or breathe the fumes of something that turns your child's hair green. Ever notice how after a summer in the pool, your bathing suit grows thin and starts to deteriorate? That's chlorine and sun breaking down the materials. You let water sit before dropping your goldfish into his cleaned bowl so that the chlorine dissipates.

Your body can absorb more chlorine in a ten-minute shower than in drinking eight glasses of the same water. Chlorinated or chemically treated and potentially contaminated water is inhaled as it turns to vapor during your shower, or it is absorbed by the skin as you soak in a hot tub of unfiltered water.

Other contaminants found in public drinking water include pesticide runoff, herbicides, and industrial by-products such as solvents. Fluoride, another potent chemical, is added to drinking water and toothpaste (in a slightly less toxic form) to strengthen teeth and limit cavities. Studies have shown that the fluoride used in water treatment contributes to the presence of toxic metals, trace amounts of radioactive isotopes, and significant levels of arsenic, a known carcinogen. You can obtain information from your local water district about what's in your water; you can also purchase a kit to test your water for chemicals.

It makes sense to do everything you can to limit your and your family's exposure to the chemicals in treated water. In the bathroom, you can improve water quality with water purification systems designed for the showerhead and at the taps of the bathtub and sink. Various filtration systems are available for your home in many sizes and price ranges. The main types of water purification systems use *carbon filters* to remove chlorine, bad taste, and pesticides; *reverse osmosis,* to remove bacteria and dissolved solids; and *UV light filters* to kill microorganisms.

Decoration

That floral shower curtain, soft towel, or cheery bath mat might look lovely and fresh, but is it? If it's made with plastic, vinyl, or synthetic fabric, it can give off harmful compounds that have been shown to cause immune-system dysfunction, allergies, and other reactions in many people. Natural, unbleached fabrics and materials are your best choice. The wealth of natural fabrics and furnishings made from organic, unbleached cotton, hemp, and linen will amaze you! Hemp naturally resists mold growth and launders very well. Try a hemp-linen blend or hemp-cotton blend for towels and shower curtains. You can periodically launder the curtain in your washing machine in hot water and hang it to dry. Certain woods, such as teak and bamboo, are naturally resistant to moisture and make good choices for furniture or flooring mats.

Instant Gratification

Artful choices

Use your imagination to come up with ways to display art in the bathroom. Works on paper or canvas will suffer from humidity, so this is not the place for valuable paintings. Collections of seashells can be displayed in glass shadow boxes, bowls of sea glass drizzled with essential oils can hold a small candle for romantic bathing. Replace a plastic soap dish with a beautiful found object such as a large scoop-shaped river rock, or use unexpected objects such as small sushi plates. Antique apothecary bottles make great containers for bath salts.

More Committed?

Buy shampoos in bulk

Avoid the waste and plastic contaminants of packaging and bottles for shampoos, conditioners, liquid hand soaps, and the like, and save on cost. You can dispense these items from bulk dispensers at health food stores using your own washable containers and decant them into beautiful metal or glass containers at home, complete with your own artistic labels.

A Truly Healthy Home

Green materials, good design

If you are building or remodeling your bathroom, research nontoxic materials and construction methods that will produce a high quality design and installation—you will reap the benefits for many years. The overall design of the bath should limit the need for overcleaning with toxic products and include good ventilation to reduce the chance of mold and moisture buildup. Pay special attention to the composition of your cabinetry as this is a major source of formaldehyde from particleboard and plywood production methods. Flooring should be from a natural source—avoid vinyl as it is exceptionally toxic. Tiles made from recycled glass and porcelain with integral color variations that make it look like real stone are available for remarkably reasonable cost. A licensed contractor, especially one versed in green materials and healthy homes, can help you make your bathroom as healthy as possible.

CHAPTER 6

Utility Areas

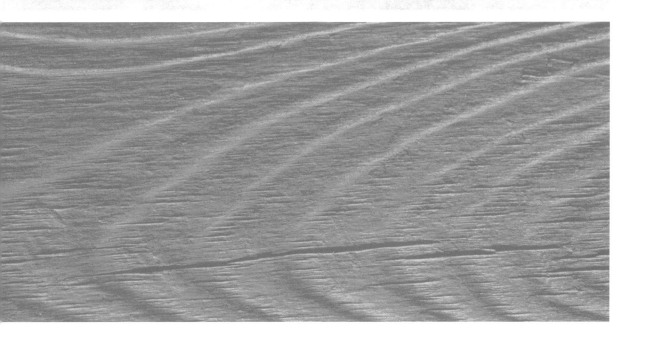

If your house was a human body, it seems the garage, basement, and laundry room could represent the "guts."

Some theories of home design (such as feng shui) and plain common sense tell you that clutter, dirt, toxins, unused items, and disorganization create chaos for the home and for your life in general. Think about the feeling you get after a major basement cleanout, a successful garage sale, or a trip to the local donation center where you purge your home of unnecessary items. Freeing yourself of material objects can be a very liberating experience. Another factor weighing on these areas of the home is that they hold the most toxic substances that we use in our daily life. These include paint and solvents, cleaning supplies and detergents, fuel for power tools, chemicals and fumes from our vehicles, pesticides, fertilizer, and many types of mold and fungus. Water heaters, furnaces, washers, and dryers can often be sources of unhealthy air.

Garages

Garages (or basements) may hold toxic chemicals and dangers, but there are simple ways to limit your exposure and decrease the quantity of toxins that enter the space. Some of the most dangerous health hazards in the garage or basement include pesticides, herbicides, paint, paint thinner, benzene, kerosene, turpentine, motor oils, and gasoline. Common chemicals include aromatic hydrocarbons in paint thinner that can cause liver and kidney damage; petroleum hydrocarbons, an ingredient of gasoline, motor oils, and benzene associated with skin and lung cancer; mineral spirits in oil-based paint that cause skin, eye, nose, throat, and lung irritation. Ketones in paint thinner may cause respiratory ailments; toluene in wood putty is highly toxic and may cause skin, kidney, liver, and central-nervous and reproductive-system damage.

Eliminate Toxic Products

For a healthy home, eliminate as many toxic chemicals as possible. This might be as simple as culling items that you no longer use. Most cities have a facility that safely disposes of toxins. Such a facility will also often accept batteries and computers as well if they can't be donated, recycled, or reused. This is also where you take old thermometers, specifically their contents: highly toxic mercury; keep this substance away from children and *never* put it in the garbage or down the drain. Dispose of excess toxic products that you don't need such as pesticides, old house paints, paint thinner, and similar items. If you are concerned about keeping paint for touch-ups, place small amounts of paint in glass jars with metal lids. (You can buy paint bottles with foam applicator tips, but plastic is not a stable material and fumes from the paint may escape.) Larger quantities of leftover paint should always be left in the original can if you need to keep it.

Find Substitutes

Make the effort to replace toxic products with safer alternatives. As you inform yourself about less toxic products, from oxygen-based cleaning agents to water-based paint and wood finishes, you'll find you need fewer harsh cleaning products or dangerous solvents. (See the section on cleaning at the back of the book.)

Be Sure All Toxic Products Are Properly Sealed and Stored

Learn to recognize flammable and toxic products and the proper ways to seal these items if you need to keep them. Paint cans will close better if you keep the top of the can clean after pouring paint or use a special spout that attaches to the can to eliminate drips. Some paint companies sell paint in screw-top containers, but because these containers are usually plastic (which breaks down faster than metal), the metal cans are still better.

Oil, paint, and other toxic products should not be stored in the basement, an attached garage, or other areas connected to the main house. Minimize your use of dangerous products (especially stronger chemicals, stripping agents, solvents, toxic craft supplies, and toxic cleaning products) and store what you still use outdoors in a shed—which itself should be in the shade but well away from species of trees and shrubs that are highly flammable—instead of in a space that you pass through daily.

Your Vehicle

If you have an electric car or hybrid, you know you've made a wise choice to limit your contribution to poor air quality and fuel usage. If not, your car is one of the main contributors to outdoor air pollution; be aware that fumes from the materials in your car, exhaust, and gasoline vapors can sneak into your home to damage indoor air quality as well. The chemical additives in fuel, including the gas that powers lawn mowers and other tools, are carcinogens. Fewer vehicles have asbestos brakes today but older vehicles still have pads that contain asbestos; this material becomes a dust particulate that can enter the air of your garage.

The location of your garage, the barrier between the garage and living quarters, and your habits will all contribute to how many of the toxic fumes and materials generated in this space make their way into your indoor environment. You can decrease the fumes your garage contains and lower the level of pollutants that enter the home.

Never let your car idle in the garage. Pull as far away from the house as is practical if you need to sit with your car running. (This also applies to idling gas-operated leaf blowers, lawn mowers, and weed whips.) Once you drive home, leave your garage door open for a while to release some of the exhaust. Make a habit of keeping the door that connects the garage and the house closed.

Don't Wash Your Car at Home

The chemicals that build up on your car, like brake dust in your wheels and spilled gas or oil from small leaks, will run off into your yard and your watershed—nearby streams, bays, or the ocean. Washing your car at a local car wash can be more water conscious if the business uses recycled water and is careful about runoff. Check with local car washes to determine their policies about water source and wastewater.

Instant Gratification

Safety stop

Check that your garage door safety stop works (with an object such as a stuffed animal or box in the way of the garage door).

Stop the drip

If you use equipment such as a gas-powered lawn mower, get a gas can dispensing spout with a trigger mechanism to eliminate drips and decrease spills by allowing you to see how much gas is being dispensed.

Avoid oil spills, promote cleaner air

Have your car checked regularly for oil leaks, keep it tuned up, and put air in the tires for cleaner emissions and efficient gas mileage as well as good maintenance. If you change your own oil, make sure oil, antifreeze, or other fluids never go on the pavement or down a storm drain; take used oil to an oil recycling center. For the sake of the planet, walk, bike, or use public transport and try to reduce unnecessary driving to help your Healthy Home be part of a healthy community.

Decrease chances for accidents by de-cluttering the garage

Create organization systems. Tools hung on a Peg-Board with outlines of the tools behind them may remind you of your high school shop class; but it is a very effective way to keep a communal space organized. Post signs in the garage or any workshop space for all family members or visitors about the safe use of hand tools, power tools, ladders, oily rags, and general safety with chemicals.

More Committed?

Seal the connection

Garages tend to be less sealed than the rest of your house and this helps to bring more fresh air into the space to dilute polluting fumes. The problem, however, is that you don't want this poorly insulated and unsealed area to allow toxic vapors to enter your living spaces. Garages that are detached are better for air quality in the home, but if your garage is attached, you will want to close off potential avenues for fumes. You can seal walls and ceilings with special paints or apply a vapor barrier. Be sure you research vapor barrier options for materials that emit no volatile organic compounds or toxic fumes. Mechanical ventilation is the best bet for your garage.

A Truly Healthy Home

Detached is best

If you are considering a remodel or addition, ask your architect, designer, or contractor for plans with a detached garage. If your garage has living space above it, you will need to be especially prudent about a vapor barrier between the ceiling of the garage and the floor of that living space.

Basements

A raw dirt basement or crawl space and even concrete basements tend to harbor mold and moisture and can even expose you to toxins such as radon gas. These areas can also provide access for pests like rats and mice.

Radon gas is a toxic by-product of some soils high in particular naturally occurring elements. This is not a common problem, but it can occur and be particularly detrimental to health. (Even stone that you order for kitchen countertops, hearths, or bathroom installations can sometimes be a source of radon). You can order a simple radon testing kit; soil from your basement is sent to the lab.

The best defense against rodents is to seal off your basement or crawl space to the best of your ability; be sure that doors and windows are well screened. Store pet food in airtight containers. See page 177 for tips on ridding your basement of rodents if it's too late for prevention.

Instant Gratification

Shut the door

Keep the door to the basement shut and weatherproof any openings leading from the basement to the main house. Shut the basement door behind you every time you make a trip down there—and remind others with a small sign.

Insulate pipes

Insulate pipes to conserve energy resources.

Appliances

Have your furnace, water heater, washer, dryer, and any other major appliances checked and serviced. Clean your forced-air vents as needed, or twice a year.

More Committed?

Add vents to the crawl space

Install vents on opposite walls of your basement to increase airflow into this space from outside, diluting toxic fumes and decreasing moisture.

Prevent pests from entering

Be sure there are no sources of food or nesting materials that pests such as rodents find attractive. Rats will create nests from any material that they can easily chew and break into small pieces. Discourage pests from entering: you can do this with mesh screen barriers over vents that still allow airflow into the basement. Check any existing vent screens for holes. Patch these with more mesh or replace; make sure the mesh is fine enough to keep out smaller pests. (See the section on cleaning at the back of the book for more information on pest control, including mice and termites.)

A Truly Healthy Home

Seal off basement soil with "rat proofing" concrete

You can have a contractor pump concrete into your basement spaces. Because concrete is often made with toxic waste by-products, you'll want to determine that the contractor is well versed in the issues of toxins that exist in most standard concrete mixes. There are many nontoxic concrete products now available. Your contractor should have extensive experience with the proper curing of concrete, because improper curing can create cracks where moisture from soil will rise up into the basement space. Seal with a nontoxic vapor barrier specifically designed for concrete, which will help prevent pests that dig through the soil, keep moisture levels down, and possibly help with radon gas if that is a problem in your area.

Laundry Rooms

Toxic Products

Most conventional laundry products contain irritants and toxic ingredients that can affect you and your family as well as the environment: these include detergents, fabric softeners, chlorine bleach, anti-cling sheets, spray starches, and spot removers. Detergents are generally derived from petrochemicals, and people sensitive to these compounds may find it hard to tolerate detergents or the fragrances they are scented with. In addition, most conventional detergents contain phosphates, which build up in streams, lakes, and waterways, causing blooms of algae that deplete the dissolved oxygen fish and other aquatic organisms need to live. Some detergents may even contain naphthalene or phenol, both hazardous substances.

Safe Substitutes for the Laundry Room

You can set up a healthy laundry area and sorting station to make laundry a more enjoyable chore. Two or three natural wicker baskets or organic cotton laundry bags will help you sort loads of lights, darks, and delicates and will wear better than plastic laundry baskets. An effective and safer alternative to using harsh detergents is to return to natural laundry soaps or use biodegradable detergents, available in health food stores. More information about toxic products and nontoxic alternatives for the laundry room can be found in the section on cleaning at the back of the book.

Instant Gratification

Safety

Keep the dryer lint screen clean. A metal wastebasket near the dryer is perfect for disposing of highly flammable lint.

More Committed?

Let the sun shine

Hang laundry to dry outside whenever you can. It will save energy resources, it's a mild form of exercise—and sunshine is a disinfectant. Nothing else makes laundry smell better, and breezes tend to take out quite a few wrinkles. If you have a dry basement or other appropriate space, a clothesline or old-fashioned wooden drying rack can work indoors, too.

A Truly Healthy Home

Vents and filters

Be sure to properly vent the laundry room to the outside and do not recirculate dryer air back into the house unless it is properly filtered with a filter system designed for this purpose.

CHAPTER 7

The Great Outdoors

Your garden, be it big or small, formal or rustic, is your connection to the natural world and, if considered carefully, a key to a more balanced and healthy home.

As you read in this chapter about the part of the world that is just outside your door, keep in mind that container gardens, windowsills, and small rooftop gardens are just as important in urban settings as the plots of vegetable crops are to rural ones or the landscaped gardens in between. So, whether you tend to a bonsai tree or a suburban yard, take pride in your connection to the earth and the peace it will bring you.

Sustainable Landscape Design

A landscape design based on organic principles is a perfect place to learn about and share with others the importance of a balanced ecosystem. No matter the style or level of formality of your garden, think of your yard as part of the healthy living environment you want to create, an extension of your home—and a natural place of transition between your living space and surviving green open space. Nature has built-in mechanisms to sustain itself and the living things of the world. Rather than looking at your yard as a place to display perfectly controlled plant specimens or exotic and unusual plants that may not grow well where you live, let your garden be a sanctuary where most of the flowers, ferns, shrubs, and trees are native to your region. In this way you can help with restoration efforts to help native birds, butterflies, and other pollinators and wildlife find the food and shelter they need to survive. You can nurture a beautiful landscape (orderly or wild according to your taste) by relying on natural processes and by planting nursery-propagated native and other appropriate hardy plants. (Nurseries, online sources, or sales at botanical gardens should be your path to acquiring native plants—they should never be removed from the wild.)

Be sure to avoid selecting landscaping plants that are invasive nonnatives such as pampas grass, Scotch or French broom (still available in nurseries in some areas), or certain ground covers. Invasive plants spread to other areas and crowd out native species (including wildflowers) in the wild.

The plants and trees native to your region have existed there for a long time, are adapted to the conditions of your particular microclimate and soil, and will flourish naturally. Organic gardening avoids use of petroleum-based or synthetic fertilizers, pesticides, or herbicides and works instead with safe methods and materials, composting, beneficial insects, and plants that give back to the soil; this approach will help your yard take care of itself. This means less maintenance, minimal watering, and no dangerous pesticides. Another concept allied with organic gardening is the approach known as permaculture, which integrates self-sustaining ecosystems with sustainable agriculture as well as efficient, ecological building design. You can make a design for edible landscaping that is beautiful and provides some of your family's food. And you can invite the birds and butterflies into your garden with native plants, shrubs, and trees that provide seeds, berries, nectar and insects as food, and nesting materials and cover—all these living things have vital roles in an ecosystem that you can help restore and nurture.

Why Choose Organic Gardening?

Industrial agriculture and conventional gardening make use of pesticides, synthetic fertilizers, genetically modified organisms (GMOs), and patented seeds, but this is far from the way flowers, crops, and other useful plants were grown in the past. The threat posed by GMOs to biodiversity around the world and the problems of soil contamination and depletion caused by conventional modern growing methods are cause for serious concern. You can contribute to a safer, more sustainable environment not only by buying organic foods and other products but also by adopting ideas for organic gardening and landscaping at home.

Make a Wish List

Create a list—or a sketch or collage—of how you envision your garden. This may include wishes such as a meandering stream, flowers in all colors of the rainbow, birds, statues, and paths—and a basketball hoop. Let your imagination go wild because many of your visions can become realities, especially once you find a common ground between basic function, aesthetics, and dreams that mean something for you and everyone else who shares your home.

Don't Be Afraid to Draw

Drawing a landscaping plan in this stage of brainstorming and exploration can be as simple as drawing basic circles and squares on a larger shape that is your property. Just plot out general concepts and focal points such as a fountain, patio, flowerbeds, veggie garden, pathways, trees, and, if needed, retaining walls. Later on, you can begin to draw a plan with dimensions to create a project outline for estimating budgets and acquiring bids from a landscaper or gardener. A landscape architect will provide dimensional drawings, but the more homework you do, the faster that will go. Whether you have a large yard or a very small space to work with, this will be an easy but eye-opening experience as you plot out potential planting areas and locations for focal points and take note of sun exposure, regular breezes, and other weather patterns.

Create a Healthy Landscaping Plan

Think about your overall outdoor area in terms of creating as many functional and pleasing spaces and planting types as possible. When you think of a yard or any outdoor space adjacent to your home, consider what's missing from the interior of your house or, for that matter, from your life: a space in which to unwind and sit quietly by yourself; a gathering space for cooking with friends and family. Is noise an issue that could be helped by hedges or a water feature, or do you feel that your space lacks privacy? Consider these points when you plan your landscape, because the enjoyment of a special place, whether in relaxation, contemplation, or in the exertion of gardening, is excellent medicine in terms of stress reduction and time well spent.

Useful Plants

Consider plants for your garden both for their beauty and for food and household use.

If you are thinking about planting trees, think about fruit trees. Lemons and limes are great to have for cleaning, preserving, flavoring, and eating. Oranges make fresh morning juice; apples and pears are healthy food and grow well in colder climates.

Lavender and rosemary are very hardy Mediterranean-climate plants that can be used for bathing, fragrance, cooking, herbal medicine, and decoration.

Chamomile creates a lush blanket of color, can be an alternative to lawn grasses, and makes a relaxing tea that helps fight insomnia.

Many culinary herbs are also health promoting; basil grows well alongside tomato plants and makes a beautiful summer salad with balsamic vinegar and fresh buffalo mozzarella.

Some ancient traditions say planting a garlic bulb—a natural antibiotic in the kitchen—near your roses makes them smell sweeter and grow more vibrantly.

A cutting garden for floral arrangements creates a special ritual that invites you outdoors to bring nature inside, always good for a sense of well-being.

The Ecosystem of an Organic Garden

You can create a naturally beneficial environment for plants by amending soil with organic matter, using mostly heirloom and native plants and only organic, non-GMO seeds and starter plants, and avoiding synthetic fertilizers or pesticides. Creating an organic landscape for your entire yard, not only for growing veggies, helps the elements of the yard work together cohesively and symbiotically. It is easier to take care of and produces stunningly beautiful results. If you choose to grow some of your own food and herbs as well as flowers, you can feel confident that you are creating healthy, nurturing, and enjoyable "fruits" of your labor.

Improve Soil Quality

Composting starts with kitchen scraps and garden clippings—you can start small. Buy or make a composting container or just create a heap, starting with twigs and alternating dry and wet plant material: no meat or grease. It is easy to find information on how to make and take care of compost so that you will have rich, clean, nourishing material to add to your garden's soil.

If you aren't ready to start a composting system, you can buy finished compost as well as organic fertilizer and soil amendments. Mulching your plant beds with dried grass cuttings, straw, or other plant material keeps moisture in the soil and helps control weeds. Ask at a local nursery what common problems exist for soil in your area. A soil sample can be tested to tell just what (organic) amendments your soil needs or what plants will do best in it.

Raised Beds

An organic raised-bed garden will give gratifying results and is ideal for growing plants from seeds, and because the plantings can be easily moved later. Keep your eyes open for unusual containers that fit your personal taste, that can be used to hold raised beds or other forms of planters. These can be anything made from a natural material that you're sure is nontoxic (stay away from containers with paint unless you can test the paint, and any type of plastic)—just look for the right size and shape to hold soil and make for a fun and artful display. You can even plant tomato plants in large coffee bean gunnysacks filled with organic soil, or sew large pieces of burlap if you can't find coffee bags.

A Garden Gathering

Make a fun day out of creating a veggie garden by having a gathering of friends and family to plant seeds in starter containers and share organic fresh food outside. Everyone can pitch in to create the garden and plant some of the seedlings and take home some planted starter containers.

Seed Saving

Look for heirloom seeds from catalogs, local gardens, and friends. Perpetuating old plant varieties helps to preserve biodiversity and thus helps create a well-balanced and hardy ecosystem. It's also a cost saver: you can save seeds from each year's organic vegetables and flowers in your garden and plant them the following year (this is not possible with patented, genetically altered commercial seeds).

Garden Toxins & Natural Alternatives

Pesticides are one of the single most important hazards in the home and garden. Around 1,400 pesticides, herbicides, and fungicides are ingredients in consumer products. Combined with other toxic substances such as solvents, pesticides are present in more than 34,000 different product formulations.

With organic practices, your garden can be protected by the health of the plants themselves, enhanced by methods such as companion planting and planting for diversity. You can learn about what plants tend to thrive together, how to avoid too much of the same thing in one spot, and other ways to help natural defenses. Beneficial insects and simple soap or garlic sprays (you can make your own) can help to deter pests. Or look for new brands of safer insecticides that use a soap and water solution to get rid of aphids or other damaging insects.

Several naturally derived pesticides exist that, in some cases, are less toxic to humans than the widely used organophosphates, carbamates, or organochlorines. Ryania kills only a few targeted species, including the European corn borer, codling moth, and cranberry fruit worm. Pyrethrum (derived from a variety of chrysanthemum) is relatively nontoxic to humans but is slightly toxic to aquatic life, so it may not be the best choice; sabadilla controls lice, leafhoppers, squash bugs, striped cucumber beetles, and chinch bugs and has low toxicity to wildlife, but it may be toxic to bees—so even the "natural" pesticides can be problematic. As more and more people understand the hazards of toxic chemicals in the home and garden, market pressure will encourage the introduction of safer products.

A more relaxed attitude of live and let live towards insects may unveil hidden delights. A wild solitary bee called the leaf-cutter bee cuts pieces from leaves and flies home with each piece rolled up in its legs to line its nest—the holes the bee leaves are not the end of the world but a sign of the fascinating life cycle of a helpful and endangered pollinator.

Instant Gratification

Ladybugs

Many garden stores sell ladybugs, voracious aphid eaters that are charming to see in your garden.

Birds

Another natural control for insects is birds. You can attract birds by hanging a bird feeder, but be sure that birdseed is unsprayed and noninvasive. It's even better for birds' health to grow native plants that provide food in the form of seeds, berries, and nectar—this avoids health problems associated with crowed feeders or fermented hummingbird nectar.

Don't be afraid

Don't discourage bats and toads—they are helpful neighbors that eat insects.

More Committed?

Hand weeding and mulching

Weeds are best controlled by hand weeding and mulching. You may have to work a little more at first, but once you help your landscape become established with naturally occurring pest management, it will thrive more readily on its own. You'll need fewer products as the ecosystem matures and supports itself. It's encouraging to know that some "weeds" are actually beneficial native plants or nonnative but edible greens that make nutritious salads if they have not been subjected to herbicides. Many weeds such as dandelions do valuable service cycling nutrients and reconditioning the soil, so they'll work for you in the ground or in the compost.

Garden hoses and irrigation pipes

See if you can find eco-friendly supplies such as alternatives to hoses, drip-irrigation hosing, and other irrigation materials made with PVC and other toxins. Too often inside the packaging of garden hoses you will find the printed warning that the product is not designed for drinking water and contains a carcinogenic substance (used for making the hose flexible). At least try to keep hoses out of the sun as much as possible, especially when they are holding water.

Stop using charcoal lighter fluid in your barbecue

Charcoal lighter fluid contains petroleum distillates. Besides being flammable and imparting a chemical taste to food, some petroleum distillates contain benzene, a known human carcinogen. A simple and much more effective alternative exists to start the backyard barbecue. A metal chimney-pipe cylinder, which holds the charcoal above a burning piece of newspaper and relies on the airflow under the charcoal to quickly bring it to glowing hot, is available at most discount stores. It quickly readies the charcoal for cooking without the chemical taste or the health and fire hazards of lighter fluid.

Sound waves

Try sound deterrents for gophers and other rodents. This is usually a matter of trial and error, because many mammals get used to the sound devices over time, but they can be an effective temporary fix as you get your garden in order. It may help to change the frequency regularly, but keep it below what is audible to human household members.

A Truly Healthy Home

Decrease the size of your lawn, switch your mower

A large, perfectly manicured lawn does not contribute to the effort to preserve biodiversity. Consider replacing some or all of your lawn with attractive native plantings that require less water and maintenance. If you do use gas-powered mowers, weed whips, or blowers, you can switch to electric, or try using hand tools for some of your garden work. Gas-powered tools are not as highly regulated as automobiles and can be very polluting to the air. If you mow your lawn weekly, you can leave the clippings as a way to insulate the grass from evaporation, meaning you need to water less. An old push mower works fine if you have a small patch of lawn and provides a workout! Herbicides are most often used to kill "unsightly" weeds in gardens and yards, and by lawn-care companies to maintain the perfect appearance of turf. Basically, the safe alternative to herbicides is simple: pull weeds by hand. There are no really safe herbicides. If you really want a lawn, select low-water grass that is appropriate to your microclimate and light conditions.

Test the soil for toxins

This may seem like something that only die-hard gardeners and farmers do, but a soil test—not for pH but for specific toxins—can be absolutely crucial for your health. One of the most potent toxins found in soil is lead. Dangerous levels of lead can be present for a variety of reasons. Arsenic has also been found in soil, especially if you have older, pressure-treated wood structures or fencing. Children and pets can be hurt and edible plants can become tainted by exposure to contaminated soil; runoff from toxins can pollute other areas. Look into bioremediation as an option for professional cleanup of some types of contamination.

Dig up some history

Investigate the history of your property. You can easily do this if you are the property owner by visiting your city or county public records or local title company. Some states now require natural hazard disclosures, but they may not tell you about past problems that were never discovered or diagnosed. Ask neighbors and people in your community (especially older folks) for any history they might have on your property. Anecdotal evidence of industrial sites, habits of previous homeowners, or even faint memories of fires or old cars sitting in the yard may be things to look for. If you rent a house or apartment, finding out about the property can still be very useful, especially if you plan to be there for a while or if you have usable yard space that your landlord allows you to work with.

Water, Peace & Quiet

Water is a precious substance that should neither be wasted nor contaminated. If your water supply comes from a faraway source, odds are an ecosystem and habitats are suffering. Learn all you can about water conservation methods and try to design your garden or landscaping with this in mind. Native plants tend to require less watering; recycling fountains avoid waste; gray-water system designs are a possibility for irrigation.

A Rain Barrel

Rainwater collection is an old idea worth reviving for watering your garden or washing the dog. Plastic and galvanized metal are unsafe for storing water, but a recycled wooden wine barrel with a spigot would serve well. Keep a lid on your barrel in dry weather to minimize pests.

Discourage Mosquitoes

Remove standing water in your yard. If you have a pond, your local insect-abatement organization will usually provide (free of charge) fish that eat mosquitoes and larvae. You can use citronella candles when you spend time outdoors, but be sure they are natural—many of these "insect deterrent" candles have synthetic fragrance and other chemicals in addition to some citrus oil.

Find Some Silence

Noise pollution can aggravate even the calmest person. For many, sensitivity to unwanted or jarring noise can produce reactions such as headaches, increased stress levels, or just pure annoyance. Some of the noise sources that you may experience might be traffic, power tools, airplanes, or even your neighbor's dog. Any sound level that is undesirable or that produces even the slightest irritation can contribute to stress or coping mechanisms that affect our physiological processes, including cardiovascular, digestive, respiratory, and endocrine processes. If you can find a place in your yard that seems especially quiet and peaceful, select this area to create a patio, seating area, or contemplation spot. Spend some time in a quiet spot of your yard at least once a day and consider making it a focal point with a pond, bench, or tree that shades a sunny spot on a warm day, or provides a place to set up a picnic or outdoor lunch.

Soften Noise Problems

If you want to decrease noise levels both inside your home and outside in your yard or garden, you can add sound buffers. Some ways to do this with your landscaping are to add thick bushes, soil mounds, or fences. A tall hedge at least two feet thick can decrease noise from areas surrounding your yard. Mounded earth added at the perimeter of your yard and planted with shrubs and perennials can help reduce traffic noise. A fence covered with vines can also help. Stay away from using stone and other hard surfaces as barriers from noises because sound will tend to bounce off of and sometimes even become magnified by a hard material.

Water Music

Another way to decrease the negative effects of noise pollution is to create a different but more pleasing sound to detract from and mask the offending noise. Look into fairly simple plans for fountains that do not waste water but keep it recirculating—these can be designed with the appearance of a small stream or spring.

You can build an "infinite fountain" with a pot or decorative container that allows water to cascade over the edge onto a bed of stones. The water falls through the rocks, through a mesh screen, and into a receiving container below the ground. The receiving container holds a pump that pushes the water back into the pot and the process starts over again. Some landscaping or rock supply sources sell large boulders or stones that have a drilled center and a shallow scoop or basin in the top. The water rises up through the boulder and it looks as though the rock is a magical natural spring! You can modify this idea with a design that lets the water run over a series of flat surfaces such as slate tiles or randomly arranged river rocks.

Switch Your Pool or Spa Treatment

You can switch from chlorine to less toxic chemical treatments. A covered pool or spa will stay cleaner; keeping your spa and pool clean of debris will decrease your need for chemicals. Make sure you shower after using the pool or spa as water treatment chemicals sitting on your skin will increase your absorption of them. Teach your children and pets not to drink pool water.

Decks & Play Equipment

Arsenic has been the main compound used to create pressure-treated lumber for fencing, outdoor decks, and even children's play structures. Although it has now been banned, you may still find arsenic in older structures or in soil that is or was adjacent to wood treated with arsenic. You can send for an arsenic test kit.

Look for materials for decking, garden furniture, or play equipment that are nontoxic (ask suppliers questions about the toxicity—in manufacturing, leaching, or out-gassing—of any type of pressure-treated wood or the new materials made of a wood fiber–plastic mix). The search for long-lasting, safe materials can be a challenge—redwood has long been considered superior for outdoor structures but its use has become an ethical problem since the rate of logging has been unsustainable and so little is left of the redwood forest ecosystem. Look for ethically harvested teak, avoiding products from unsustainable logging of rain forests—you may do best to hire a local woodworker to help you decide on materials and who can make what you want, preferably from recycled, salvaged, good-quality wood.

Resources

Nontoxic Cleaning

This section provides information on cleaning products, from benign to dangerous. It describes unhealthy chemical ingredients, what purpose they serve, and some of the harm they can do to you and the planet, including effects on air and water quality in the environment. The toxins used in many products affect humans and other living creatures—this section suggests safer alternatives, with additional information on household pests.

You can refer to the information in this section when it's cleaning day for any area of your Healthy Home.

Keeping Your Home Clean and Safe

Our great-grandmothers did not have the vast array of chemical cleaning products that are available to us today. In past generations, simple household staples such as baking soda, vinegar, and lemon juice were used (in combination with strong arms and more time spent doing housekeeping) to keep our homes clean and safe. Although we certainly have less time to spend cleaning house these days—and a desire to get the job done quickly is understandable—some contemporary, conventional products are not worth the danger they pose to our health.

We worry about bacteria and germs but trust that the products that remove offensive organisms won't harm us (or the food that touches a counter just scrubbed with a chemical cleaning product). Unfortunately, this may not be the case.

Dangers in Conventional Cleaning Products

Drain cleaners, oven cleaners, toilet bowl cleaners, and any product containing ammonia or chlorine bleach are exceptionally dangerous poisons. Sodium hypochlorite is found in chlorine bleach and, if mixed with ammonia, releases toxic chloramine gas. Short-term exposure may cause mild asthmatic symptoms or more serious respiratory problems. The phenol and cresol used in disinfectants are corrosive and can cause diarrhea, fainting, dizziness, and kidney and liver damage. Another common chemical, nitrobenzene, is found in furniture and floor polishes and can cause skin discoloration, shallow breathing, and vomiting and is associated with cancer and birth defects.

Other common products likely to contain irritants or toxic ingredients include carpet cleaners, room deodorizers, laundry detergents and softeners, anti-cling dryer sheets, mold and mildew cleaners, spot removers, and mothballs. Perchloroethylene or 1-1-1 trichloroethane solvents (in spot removers and carpet cleaners) can cause liver and kidney damage if ingested; perchloroethylene is an animal carcinogen and suspected human carcinogen. Naphthalene (used in mothballs) may damage eyes, blood, liver, kidneys, skin, and the central nervous system and is a suspected human carcinogen. Paradichlorobenzene (another chemical used for mothballs) can harm the central nervous system, liver, and kidneys. Hydrochloric acid or sodium acid sulfate in toilet bowl cleaner can burn the skin or cause vomiting, diarrhea, and stomach burns if swallowed and can cause blindness if inadvertently splashed in the eyes. Residues from fabric softeners, as well as the fragrances commonly used in them, can be irritating to susceptible people; dangerous ingredients in spray starch may include formaldehyde, phenol, or pentachlorophenol. In addition, any aerosolized particle, including cornstarch, may irritate the lungs.

Safe Substitutes for Cleaning Your Home

One shelf of simple and relatively safe ingredients can be used to perform most home cleaning chores. All that's needed is knowledge of how different ingredients work and how they should or should not be combined to get the cleaning power needed for a specific job. You can purchase many nontoxic, biodegradable, and non-petrochemically derived products in your local health food store. As you educate yourself about products, be sure that you review all ingredients on the label (sometimes trademark laws and industry standards allow a separate list of "inert" ingredients by percentage). What the law considers inert is up for debate, as are the potential side effects of these ingredients for some individuals. Put more trust in a company that lists everything in its product and tells you how the ingredients are derived. Many washing products have sudsing agents that are petrochemically derived and thus involved with pollution in the environment and in your home. Safer alternatives come from plant sources—many products now proudly market this.

Ask your older relatives about the cleaning practices of past generations. This could be a great activity to engage in with your children as it reconnects us with simple, inexpensive ways of maintaining a healthy household. The following is a list of some simple, time-tested ingredients for safe cleaning.

Baking soda (sodium bicarbonate) has a number of useful properties. It can scrub shiny materials without scratching, deodorize, extinguish grease fires, and neutralize acid. It can be used as a deodorizer in the refrigerator and on carpets and upholstery. It can help clear and deodorize drains. You can use it to clean and polish aluminum, chrome, jewelry, plastic, porcelain, silver, stainless steel, and tin and to soften fabrics and remove certain stains. Baking soda can soften hard water and makes a relaxing bath time soak; it can be used as an underarm deodorant and as a toothpaste, too.

Borax is a naturally occurring mineral, soluble in water. It can deodorize, inhibit the growth of mildew and mold, boost the cleaning power of soap or detergent, remove stains, and be used with attractants such as sugar to kill cockroaches.

Cornstarch can be used to clean windows, polish furniture, shampoo carpets and rugs, and starch clothes.

Lemon juice, which contains citric acid, is a deodorant and can be used to clean glass and remove stains from aluminum, clothes, and porcelain. It works as a mild lightener or bleach when used with sunlight.

Soap (*not* detergent): Castile soap can be used as a shampoo or as a body soap. Olive-oil based soap is gentlest to the skin. An all-purpose liquid soap can be made by dissolving the old ends of natural bar soap (or grated slivers of bar soap) in warm water.

Steel wool is an abrasive strong enough to remove rust and stubborn food residues and to scour barbecue grills without chemicals.

TSP (trisodium phosphate, a mixture of soda ash and phosphoric acid) is toxic if swallowed but can be used on many jobs that would normally require much more caustic and poisonous chemicals, such as cleaning drains or removing old paint, and it does not create any fumes.

Vinegar is a mild acid and can dissolve mineral deposits and grease, remove traces of soap, mildew, or wax buildup, polish some metals, and deodorize. Vinegar can clean brick or stone and is an ingredient in some natural carpet cleaning formulas. Use vinegar to clean out coffeepots and to shine windows without streaking. Vinegar is normally used in a solution with water, but it can be used straight.

Washing soda (or SAL soda, sodium carbonate decahydrate, a mineral) is available from drugstores. It cuts stubborn grease on grills, broiler pans, and ovens. It can be used instead of laundry detergent, and it softens hard water.

Fresh Air and Green Cleaning

For common household tasks, try these nontoxic strategies.

Freshen the air: Open your windows while you clean and anytime you can to let in fresh air. Distribute partially filled dishes of vinegar around the kitchen to combat unpleasant cooking odors; boil cinnamon and cloves in a pan of water to scent the air; sprinkle 1/2 cup borax in the bottom of garbage pails or diaper pails to inhibit mold and bacterial growth that can cause odors; rub vinegar on hands before and after slicing onions to remove the smell; use bowls of naturally scented potpourri to sweeten inside air.

All-purpose cleaner can be made from a vinegar-and-salt mixture or from 4 tablespoons baking soda dissolved in 1 quart warm water.

Disinfectants will reduce the number of harmful bacteria on a surface, but no surface treatment will completely eliminate germs. Try regular cleaning with soap and hot water. Or mix 1/2 cup borax into 1 gallon of hot water to disinfect and deodorize. Isopropyl alcohol is an excellent disinfectant, but use gloves and keep it away from children.

Drain cleaner: Try a plunger first, though not after using any commercial drain opener. To open clogs, pour 1/2 cup baking soda down the drain, add 1/2 cup white vinegar, and cover the drain. Do not use this method after trying a commercial drain opener—the combination can create dangerous fumes.

Floor cleaner and polish can be as simple as a few drops of vinegar in the cleaning water to remove soap traces. For wood floors, apply a thin coat of equal parts light oil and vinegar and rub in well. For painted wooden floors, mix 1 teaspoon washing soda into 1 gallon hot water. For brick and stone tiles, use 1 cup white vinegar in 1 gallon water and rinse with clear water.

Metal cleaners and polishes differ for each metal. Clean aluminum with a solution of cream of tartar and water. Brass may be polished with a soft cloth dipped in a solution of lemon and baking soda or of vinegar and salt. Polish chrome with baby oil, vinegar, or aluminum foil with the shiny side out. Clean tarnished copper by boiling the article in a pot of water with 1 tablespoon salt and 1 cup white vinegar, or try differing mixtures of salt, vinegar, baking soda, lemon juice, and cream of tartar. Clean gold with toothpaste, pewter with a paste of salt, vinegar, and flour. Silver can be polished by boiling it in a pan lined with aluminum foil and filled with water to which a teaspoon each of baking soda and salt have been added. Stainless steel can be cleaned with undiluted white vinegar.

Oven cleaner: Sprinkle baking soda on a moist surface and scrub with steel wool.

Scouring powder can be made from baking soda or dry table salt. Or try Bon-Ami Cleaning Powder or Bon-Ami Polishing Cleaner.

Toilet bowl cleaner can be made from baking soda and vinegar, or borax and lemon juice. Avoid using chlorine bleach, which is toxic to the environment and particularly dangerous in combination with other substances.

Tub and tile cleaner can be as easy as rubbing in baking soda with a damp sponge and rinsing, or wiping with vinegar first and following with baking soda as a scouring powder.

Window and glass cleaner: To avoid streaks, don't wash windows when the sun is shining. Use a vinegar-and-water solution, cornstarch-vinegar-and-water solution, or lemon juice and water. Wipe with newspaper, unless you are sensitive to the inks in newsprint.

Safe Substitutes for Laundry Products

Try switching from conventional laundry detergents, fabric softeners, and dryer sheets to nontoxic products, including nonchlorine oxygen bleach and essential oil–infused laundry liquid and dryer sachets. Soap is an effective, milder alternative and leaves items such as diapers softer than detergent can. For cotton and linen, use soap to soften water. One-half to three-quarters of a cup of baking soda will leave clothes soft and smelling fresh. Silks and wools may be hand washed with mild soap or a protein shampoo, down or feathers with mild soap or baking soda.

A cup of vinegar added to the wash can help keep colors bright. DO NOT combine vinegar with chlorine bleach—never combine ammonia or bleach (they are present in many commercial products as well) with other cleaners or vinegar as the resulting fumes can be very toxic.

For synthetic fabrics or blends (including most no-iron fabrics)—if you haven't culled synthetics from your closet—there are biodegradable detergents on the market that do not contain phosphates, fragrances, or harsh chemicals. They are readily available at some grocery stores, health food stores, online, or by mail order.

As you shop for cleaner, healthier laundry substitutes, you may find that some of these products give great results and smell lovely but are expensive. If that poses a problem or if you prefer not to buy a new plastic bottle every few months, buy simple liquid soap that is pure castile or coconut-derived soap from bulk sections at whole food stores and scent it yourself with essential oil. A drop will do, and you can vary the fragrance depending on what you are washing, the time of year, or your mood!

Household Pests

Prevention

Sometimes question of toxins arises when dealing with ants, mice, and other unwelcome visitors. The best offense for pests inside your home is a good defense. The first step is to make the house—especially the kitchen—unattractive to pests by cleaning up food spills immediately, keeping hard-to-reach areas reasonably clean, and removing clutter that can hide pests. Store foods attractive to pests, such as flour, in the refrigerator. Water attracts pests, so leaky faucets and pipes should be promptly repaired. To discourage mosquitoes, avoid leaving even very shallow sources of standing water outside. Doors and windows should be well screened. Clothes should be regularly cleaned and aired and properly stored in paper or cardboard boxes sealed against moths.

Rodents

Mouse and rat traps are an alternative to poisons; there are humane, nonlethal traps if you can manage the aspect of safely releasing the rodents in open areas. Poison baits are especially dangerous as it is common for a poisoned mouse or rat to become extremely dehydrated after eating bait. The animal will search out water and become disoriented. This is often when a predator such as a hawk, a bobcat, or an owl—or even your household cat or dog—may hunt and catch the toxic animal and ingest the poison, which thus damages wildlife or domestic animals.

Insects

Try to avoid killing beneficial insects. If a bee swarm lodges in your attic or under the eaves—or if you are bothered by nests of stinging insects that are pollinators such as yellow jacket or other wasps—look up beekeepers in your phone book. They will safely remove and relocate honeybees and may have nontoxic or not-so-toxic strategies for the bees' less sweet cousins.

A number of nontoxic substances can be used to repel troublesome insects. Highly fragrant or volatile herbs, spices, or oils such as citrus or cedar oil, powdered red chili pepper, peppermint, bay leaves, cloves, lavender, rosemary, tobacco, or peppercorns repel various types of insects, including clothes moths.

Noxious insects can be trapped and killed without resorting to dangerous chemicals: generally a poison nontoxic to humans is mixed with a food that insects find attractive and spread in the infested area. Examples are oatmeal (attractive) and plaster of paris (poisonous to bugs), or cocoa powder and flour (attractive) and borax (poisonous to bugs). Old-fashioned flypaper—not a hanging strip of insecticide—is an effective trap.

To deter specific house pests, try these solutions:

Ants: Sprinkle powdered red chili pepper, paprika, dried peppermint, or borax where the ants are entering.

Cockroaches: Mix by stirring and sifting 1 ounce TSP, 6 ounces borax, 4 ounces sugar, and 8 ounces flour. Spread on floor of infested area. Repeat after 4 days and again after 2 weeks.

Fleas: Feed your pet brewer's yeast in powder mixed with food or by tablets. Leaves of eucalyptus or California bay laurel in a pet's sleeping area help repel fleas.

Moths: Air clothes well in the sun; store in airtight containers. Scatter sachets of lavender, cedar chips, bay leaves, or dried tobacco in with clothing.

Rats and mice: Again, prevention may be the best cure. Holes in exterior or interior walls should be closed off and storage spaces kept orderly. Garbage should be kept tightly covered. To catch rodents, the most efficient system is the oldest: a cat. Next best are mouse or rat traps.

Termites: Any wooden parts of the house should be at least 18 inches off the ground, as subterranean termites cannot tolerate being exposed to air and light. They have to build easily visible mud tunnels to get at available wood. Most houses have only about an 8-inch clearance between wooden parts and the ground, which makes the wood vulnerable. Metal shields may help discourage termites, but they cannot prevent infestations. To treat existing termite infestations, there are a few nontoxic alternatives: call and research termite products in your area.

To a Healthy Home

You can apply these tips on green cleaning and pest control to help ensure that your entry, living areas, kitchen, bedrooms, and other spaces as well as your yard are healthy, safe, nontoxic, and beautiful.

Glossary

Aerosol - a suspension of small liquid or solid particles in gas

Biodegradable - waste material composed primarily of natural elements, able to be broken down and absorbed into the ecosystem (wood—yes, plastic—no)

Carcinogen - a chemical agent that is capable of causing cancer

Chlorination by-products - cancer-causing chemicals created when chlorine from industrial processing or water disinfection combines with dirt and organic matter in water

Chlorine - a highly reactive halogen element, used most often in the form of a pungent gas to disinfect drinking water

Chlorofluorocarbons (CFCs) - artificially created chemical compounds, used primarily for cooling in refrigerators and air conditioners. These have been found to damage the ozone layer, which protects the earth from excessive ultraviolet radiation

Dioxin - a chemical by-product formed during manufacturing and incineration of other chemicals. It is the most potent animal carcinogen ever tested. In humans, symptoms are severe weight loss, liver problems, kidney problems, birth defects, and death

Eco-label - a seal or logo indicating that a product has met a set of environmental or social standards

GMOs - genetically modified organisms (plants or animals bred to carry genetic material of unrelated species, such as salmon with pig genes)

Green - supporting preservation of environmental quality

Green design - a design that conforms to environmentally sound principles of building, materials, and energy through the use of elements such as solar panels, skylights, and recycled building materials

Healthy - sound and balanced, in accordance with environment and surroundings, free of pathogens or contamination

Humane - with compassionate consideration for humans and animals

Immune-system dysfunction - malfunction of normal immunity

Mutagen - something that causes a change in the structural DNA of a living organism that can be passed on to future generations

Natural - in accordance with or determined by nature; conforming to the ordinary course of nature

Neuro-toxin - a toxic chemical that causes adverse effects on the peripheral nervous system. Symptoms include muscle weakness, loss of sensation and motor control, tremors, cognitive alterations, and autonomic nervous system dysfunction

Nitrogen oxides - harmful gases (contributing to acid rain and global warming) released as by-products of fossil fuel combustion

Noise pollution - environmental degradation from harmful or stress-producing noise

Off-gas - release of (often toxic) gasses as by-products from synthetic materials

Organic - produced without artificial inputs, such as synthetic pesticides and fertilizers; anything claiming to be organic must be certified by a government organization such as the USDA

Organochlorines - organic compounds that contain chlorine (e.g., DDT, PCBs) can be toxic to animal and human life

Pesticides - chemical agents used to destroy pests

Petrochemical - a product derived from petroleum

Plastics - durable and flexible synthetic-based products; these are difficult to recycle and pose toxicity problems

Recycling - process of collecting, sorting, and reprocessing old material into usable raw materials

Reduce - the concept of reducing consumption in order to avoid having to reuse or recycle later

Reuse - cleaning and/or refurbishing an old product for reuse

Sick building syndrome - a human health condition characterized by lingering infections caused by exposure to contaminants within a building as a result of poor ventilation

Sustainable - able to last over a long period of time without depleting or permanently damaging natural resources, air and water quality, soil conditions, climate

Sustainable communities - communities capable of maintaining their present levels of growth without damaging effects

Tap water - drinking water monitored (and often filtered) for protection against contamination and available for consumption within the home

Toxic - poisonous

VOCs - volatile organic compounds (toxic carbon-based or petrochemical compounds that vaporize at relatively low temperature)

Waterborne contaminants - unhealthy chemicals, microorganisms (like bacteria), or radiation found in tap water

Water filters - substances (such as charcoal) or fine membrane structures used to remove impurities from water

Healthy Home Resources

Organizations

Center for Food Safety
(202) 547-9359
www.centerforfoodsafety.org

EcoSource Mississauga
(905) 274-6222
Clarke Hall, 2nd Floor
161 Lakeshore Road West
Mississauga, Ontario
L5H 1G3 Canada
www.ecosource.ca
Environmental education for
Canadians

Green Resource Center
(510) 845-9503
1931 Center Street
Berkeley, CA 93939
www.greenresourcecenter.org
Advises homeowners and businesses
on sustainable and environmentally
responsible building practices

iGreenBuild.com
(714) 279-7933
www.igreenbuild.com
Provides information about sustainable design and construction

Natural Resources Defense Council
(212) 727-2700
40 West 20th Street
New York, NY 10011
www.nrdc.org

Sierra Club
(415) 977-5500
85 Second Street, 2nd Floor
San Francisco, CA 94105
www.sierraclub.org

Home Goods

Abundant Earth
(888) 513-2784
762 West Park Avenue
Port Townsend, WA 98368
www.abundantearth.com
A range of eco-friendly products for
people and pets

Advanced Water Filters
(800) 453-4206
4205 N. Winfield Scott Plaza, Suite 5
Scottsdale, AZ 85251
www.advancedwaterfilters.com
Filters for drinking water and
the bath

Allergy Buyers Club
(888) 236-7321
486 Totten Pond Road
Waltham, MA 02451
www.allergybuyersclub.com
Air filters and hypoallergenic
products

Bamboo Mountain
(415) 883-1300
354 Bel Marin Keys Blvd, Suite L
Novato, CA 94949
www.bamboomountain.com
Renewable bamboo flooring

Benjamin Moore & Co.
(800) 344-0400
www.benjaminmoore.com
Look for the low-odor, low-VOC
Eco Spec paints

Earthweave Carpet Mills, Inc.
(706) 278-8200
P.O. Box 6120
Dalton, GA 30722
www.earthweave.com
All-natural, biodegradable carpets
and rugs

Eco Timber
(415) 258-8454
www.ecotimber.com
Ecologically sound wood flooring

EL: Environmental Language
(847) 382-9285
425 Park Barrington Drive
Barrington, IL 60010
www.el-furniture.com
Modern, nontoxic furniture

Gaiam
(877) 989-6321
www.gaiam.com
Health-care and personal products

HealthyHome.com
(727) 322-1058
2894 22nd Avenue North
Saint Petersburg, FL 33713
www.healthyhome.com
Everything from cleaning supplies
to pet goods

Innovations Wallcoverings
(800) 227-8053
150 Varick Street, 9th floor
New York, NY 10013
www.innovationsusa.com
Natural, renewable, and recyclable
wallcoverings

InterfaceFlor
(866) 281-3507
www.interfaceflor.com
Eco-friendly, modular carpets
and rugs

Johns Manville
(800) 654-3103
www.jm.com
Ecologically sound, nontoxic
building materials

Lifekind
(800) 284-4983
P.O. Box 1774
Grass Valley, CA 95945
www.lifekind.com
Organic and naturally safer
products

LIVOS
www.livos.co.uk
Low-VOC wood stains and finishes

NaturaLawn of America
(301) 694-5440
1 East Church Street
Frederick, MD 21701
www.nl-amer.com
Organic-based lawn care

Real Goods
(800) 762-7325
360 Interlocken Blvd, Suite 300
Broomfield, CO 80021
www.realgoods.com
Renewable and energy-saving
products

Seventh Generation
(802) 658-3773
212 Battery Street, Suite A
Burlington, VT 05401-5281
www.seventhgeneration.com
Cleaning and paper products

Solatube International, Inc.
(800) 966-7652
2210 Oak Ridge Way
Vista, CA 92081
www.solatube.com
Skylights that redirect and focus
natural sunlight on interiors

Vivaterra
(800) 233-6011
www.vivaterra.com
Organic, artisan-made, and earth-
friendly household goods

Bibliography

Paula Baker Laporte, Erica Elliot, M.D., and John Banta, *Prescriptions for a Healthy House: A Practical Guide for Architects, Builders and Homeowners,* New Society Publishers, 2001.

Alan Berman, *Your Naturally Healthy Home: Stylish, Safe, Simple,* Rodale, 2001.

Christopher Bryson, *The Fluoride Deception,* Seven Stories Press, 2004.

Ros Byam Shaw, *Naturally Modern,* Harry N. Abrams Inc., 2000.

Daniel D. Chiras, *The Natural House: A Complete Guide to Healthy, Energy-Efficient, Environmental Homes,* Chelsea Green Publishing Company, 2000.

Debra Lynn Dadd, *Home Safe Home: Protecting Yourself and Your Family from Everyday Toxics and Harmful Household Products in the Home,* J. P. Tarcher, 2005.

Debra Lynn Dadd, *The Nontoxic Home & Office: Protecting Yourself and Your Family from Everyday Toxics and Health Hazards,* G. P. Putnam's Sons, 1992.

Angela Dean, *Green by Design: Creating a Home for Sustainable Living,* Gibbs Smith, 2003.

Laura Fronty & Yves Duronsoy, *A Well-Kept Home: Household Traditions and Simple Secrets from a French Grandmother,* Universe, 1999.

Angela Hobbs, *The Sick House Survival Guide: Simple Steps to Healthier Homes,* New Society Publishers, 2003.

Lynn Lawson, *Staying Well in a Toxic World: Understanding Environmental Illness, Multiple Chemical Sensitivities, Chemical Injuries, Sick Building Syndrome,* Lynnword Press, 1993.

Gina Lazenby, *The Healthy House Book: Using Feng Shui to Organize Your Home and Transform Your Life,* The Lyons Press, 2000.

Linda Mason Hunter, *The Healthy Home: An Attic-to-Basement Guide to Toxin-Free Living,* Pocket Books, 1990 (Authors Guild Backinprint.com 2000).

Jennifer Roberts, *Good Green Homes: Creating Better Homes for a Healthier Planet,* Gibbs Smith, 2003.

Jerome Schofferman, M.D., *What To Do for a Pain in the Neck: The Complete Program for Neck Relief,* Simon & Schuster, 2001

Danny Seo, *Conscious Style Home: Eco-Friendly Living for the 21st Century,* St. Martin's Press, 2001.

David Steinman and Samuel S. Epstein, *The Safe Shopper's Bible: A Consumer's Guide to Nontoxic Household Products,* John Wiley & Sons, 1995.

Athena Thompson, *Homes That Heal and Those That Don't,* New Society Publishers, 2004.

Judi Vance, *Beauty to Die For: The Cosmetic Consequences,* ProMotion Publishing, 1998.

Credits

Thank you to the following people for contributing their homes, locations, props, and insight to this project:

Caner House
Arkin Tilt architects
PAGES 2, 45, 76, 117, 122, 142, 145, 146, 157

Glide House
MIchelle Kaufman Designs
www.glidehouse.com
www.mkd-arc.com
PAGES 13, 91, 97, 132, 137, 151

Michael Sainato and Iris in't Hout
Joseph Eichler
Design by A. Quincy Jones and Frederick Emmons
PAGES 26, 40, 57, 64, 69, 86, 166

Neal House
Fran Halperin, Architect
Halperin & Christ
PAGES 20, 31, 43, 51, 84, 106, 112

Nelson-Roy House
Nilus de Matran-designer
PAGES 8, 36, 71, 108, 127

Stewart + Brown Clothing
www.stewartbrown.com
PAGES 76, 142

Painting by Gretchen Kish Neal
www.kishnealstudios.com
PAGE 106

Matt Reoch of Birdman Locations
Neal House, Nelson-Roy House
www.birdmaninc.com
PAGE 16, 20, 30, 42, 50, 84, 106, 112

Acknowledgments

This book was inspired and nurtured by the stories of many people who are impacted by chemical sensitivity, illness, and a desire to make the world a cleaner place. I am grateful for my exposure to a multitude of innovative designers and companies who are doing the right thing for human health and our precious planet.

I'd like to thank Lisa Campbell for being so supportive and open during the process of writing the book. This project could not have been possible without her guidance and words of encouragement.

I owe immense gratitude to my agent, Kristy Savicke, for seeing the opportunity to share this notion of sustainability, environmentalism, and healthy living with a broad audience. She has proven to me that people are eager for knowledge and excited about change.

My clients have always been a source of great learning, and I am very grateful to those who have been trusting, collaborative, and ready to open their lives to me so that we could work together so successfully over the years.

I am so thankful and proud to have been able to collaborate on this book with Celery Design, whose innovative and thoughtful design treatment makes for pleasurable reading. I am also blessed to have had photographer Thayer Allyson Gowdy's insightful choices and astounding talent to showcase the breadth and possibilities for a beautiful Healthy Home.

I am surrounded by a loving and outdoorsy family: years of play, travel, and adventure in nature have helped to make me respectful and in awe of the natural world. This has inspired my work, my lifestyle, and a devotion to creating beauty without damaging our environment.

I would also like to thank my loving husband, Casey. He creates balance in our lives with his strength and caring through all of my creative endeavors and challenges.

It is my hope that this book will be a starting point for change in the lives of people who read it. It is meant to open your mind to yearn for more knowledge. I encourage creativity, getting back to basics, and permission to pamper yourself while you embark on a journey towards a healthy home, body, and lifestyle!

Biographies

Kimberly Rider is the founder of Atmosphera, an interior design firm dedicated to blending sustainable materials and modern style for homeowners, developers, and business owners. Her ability to deliver innovative, healthy home designs on tight budgets has earned her a loyal following across the country. Kimberly has appeared as the featured designer on HGTV's *Curb Appeal,* where she received rave reviews from viewers. Kimberly lives and works in Marin County, California. Learn more about her at www.atmospherahome.com.

Thayer Allyson Gowdy

Thayer Allyson Gowdy's photographs can be seen in *Real Simple, InStyle Home,* and *Health,* as well as the book *Nest for Two,* published by Chronicle Books. She lives in San Francisco, California.

Leather Garment Care

A leather garment should be treated as any other fine garment, with a few exceptions:

1. Do not store the garment on a wire hanger. Always use a wide hanger to maintain the garment's shape.

2. Do not store leather garments in plastic bags or in a hot, bright, or damp room. Excess dryness may cause the leather to crack and moisture can cause mildew. Consider using cold storage during the summer months.

3. If a leather garment gets wet, allow it to air dry naturally, since quick drying near a radiator will cause the leather to dry out and crack.

4. A new leather garment can be pre-treated with a stain-repellent finish, which will help prevent stains from occurring.

5. Leather cleaners and conditioners are available in retail outlets to help restore leather garments to their original state after repeated wear. However, an excess buildup of these products can clog the pores in the leather, inhibiting the skin's ability to

breathe. Apple Brand Leather Care® is a light cleaner and conditioner that is easy to use and effective. Lexol® Brand cleaner and conditioner also is a good product. Note: All cleaners should be tested for staining on a small hidden area of the garment, for example, near the hem or under them collar.

6. Do not apply pins or adhesive tape to the surface of leather garments.

7. Avoid spraying perfume and hairspray directly onto a leather garment. In general, do not allow a garment to become exceedingly soiled, as this may cause permanent damage.

8. Do not attempt to remove difficult stains. Contact a qualified professional leather cleaner.

9. A hem can be fixed by applying a small amount of rubber cement to the area.

10. Iron a leather or suede garment by placing a heavy brown paper bag on top of it; use a low setting, with no steam.

11. Expect some color and texture changes after professional dry cleaning, even when performed by qualified professionals.

12. Garments may shrink after professional dry cleaning but will stretch out again with wear.

13. Wipe off dust and dirt on a leather garment with a soft dry sponge or cloth. Buy a special suede brush and buffing block to clean the surface of nu-buck and suede.

14. Only trust a professional leather dry cleaner to clean a leather garment. (See Appendix C, Resource Directory, for a list of leather cleaners.)

15. Do not send leather garments to the neighborhood dry cleaner unless they can demonstrate that large volumes of these garments are cleaned on a regular basis. Most local dry cleaners know a lot more about textiles than leathers. Do not consider cleaning a leather garment at a "coin op" dry cleaning location.

16. Women should consider wearing scarves when wearing delicate, difficult-to-clean leather garments, as scarves protect garments from cosmetics and body oils.

17. To remove a small minor stain use a large pencil e[...] after this process has been tested on the inner, une[...] of the garment to ensure the eraser does not dam[...]

18. If a garment becomes wrinkled, put it on a hang[...] pull the wrinkles out without significantly stretchi[...] this fails, try to press the garment with an iron. Fi[...] the garment is totally dry. Place a heavy brown pa[...] the garment and keep the iron constantly mo[...] paper. Set the iron on its lowest heat setting. Ne[...] when ironing.

Trade Organizations, Shows, Publications, and Schools

Trade Organizations

The leather apparel industry has two main trade organizations, Leather Industries of America and the Leather Apparel Association.

LEATHER INDUSTRIES OF AMERICA

Suite 515
1000 Thomas Jefferson Street, NW
Washington, DC 20007
202-342-8086
Fax: 202-342-9063

For over seventy-five years, the Leather Industries of America (LIA) has represented the leather industry in the United States. Its membership is comprised of:

1. Leather Members, that is, tanners and sellers of United States leather
2. General Members, that is, United States hide and skin suppliers, chemical companies, machinery suppliers, product manufacturers, and other related companies
3. Foreign general members

The LIA provides technical, educational, environmental, statistical, and marketing services to its members. Its legal team works in Washington for Congressional and regulatory action to abolish trade restrictions, promote leather exports, and promote cost-efficient environmental regulations.

Through its publications, the LIA keeps its members informed. Its publications include:

1. Newsbreak
2. Technical Bulletin
3. Leather Industries Statistics
4. Membership Directory and Buyer's Guide and Calendar of Events
5. Dictionary of Leather Terminology
6. Leather Facts
7. Trade Practices for Proper Packer Cattlehide Delivery

The LIA sponsors four shows annually, which include:

1. The Tag Show (New York) at the International Fashion Fabric Exhibition (IFFE)
2. LIA Pavilions at the Hong Kong Trade Fair (Hong Kong)
3. Semaine Internationale du Cuir (Paris)
4. ANPIC (Mexico)

LIA RESEARCH LABORATORY
University of Cincinnati
P.O. Box 210014
Cincinnati, OH 45221-0014
513-556-1200
Fax: 513-556-2377

The LIA Research Laboratory at the University of Cincinnati is staffed by highly trained technical and scientific personnel. The laboratory is involved in researching industrial and environmental issues, monitoring government regulations, training technical personnel, and providing technical service and consultation.

The laboratory offers testing services to evaluate leather products for defects. It tests in accordance with ALCA, ASTM, EPA, ISO, WEF, Federal Test Method Standards, and the Upholstery Test Method Standards. The laboratory is certified under the U.S. Department of Defense Qualified Laboratory List #18415. If a customer or manufacturer has problems with skins or with a garment, the product can be sent to the lab. After specifying the problem, it will be tested. All test results are confidential.

THE LEATHER APPAREL ASSOCIATION

Suite 403
19 West 21st Street
New York, NY 10010
212-727-1215
Fax: 212-727-1218

The Leather Apparel Association (LAA), established in 1990, is a nonprofit organization comprised of leather retailers, manufacturers, tanners, cleaners, and others in the leather apparel industry. Its goal is to promote the leather apparel industry through aggressive marketing, which in turn increases sales and public awareness of leather garments.

PROGRAMS.   The organization sponsors a number of ongoing programs, including:

1. LAA Hotline
    - Consumers and reporters look to the LAA as the authority in leather apparel.
    - The LAA hotline (212-924-8895, Fax: 212-727-1218) acts as a referral service for its members.

2. LAA Press Kits and Fashion Shows
    • Promote to the press the latest trends in leather apparel.
3. Consumer Brochures
    • Advice is provided on how to clean and care for leather garments. These brochures are distributed to customers in stores by direct mail.
4. Market Research and Services
5. Hangtags: Guidelines for Proper Leather Garment Care
6. Leather Sales Training Handbooks
7. International Trade Policy and Lobbying

PUBLICATIONS.   The LAA offers numerous publications for both the trade and consumer. Some examples include:

Best in Leather
An animal catalog featuring leather fashions manufactured by association members beginning at the fall wholesale season. Seen by over 18,000 members.

Your Guide to Leather
A consumer brochure that educates the leather consumer about the care and cleaning of leather garments; provides shopping tips and contains a glossary of leather terms.

Handbook for Selling Leather Apparel
A brochure that educates the leather seller in all aspects of leather garments, such as leather terms, manufacturing, quality evaluation, and the care and cleaning of leather garments.

Bimonthly newsletter
Keeps members abreast of domestic and international issues, LAA activities, trends, and business developments as they occur:

Shows

CALENDAR OF EVENTS

Name of Event	Details
Panamerican Leather Fair (T/S)	Miami Beach Convention Center Miami, Florida February
Asia Pacific Fair (T/S)	Hong Kong Convention Center Hong Kong March/April For raw materials and manufacturing and fashion products
Le Semaine du Cuir (T/S)	Parc d' Expo Paris—Nord Villepointe Paris, France September
The New England Leather Components Shows (T/S)	The World Trade Center Boston, MA January and August
Intersic (T/S)	Paris—Nord Villepoint Paris, France September
The Salon de la Maroquinerie (P)	Porte de Versailles Paris, France September
Igedo Dusseldorf (P/S)	Fairgrounds Dusseldorf, Germany September
TAG Leather Show (P/S) at The International Fashion Fabric Exhibition	Jacob Javits Center New York, NY October
Anpic (T/S)	Centro de Exposiciones Leon. Gto., Mexico February

KEY: P = Products   T = Tanners   S = Suppliers

Name of Event	Details
Mipel (P)	Milan Fairground Milan, Italy October
Lineapelle (T/S)	Piazza d. Const. Bologna, Italy November and May
Leather Expo (T/P/S)	Expo Centre Sharjah, United Arab Emirates November
Pielespana (T/S)	Barcelona, Spain January
Europe/Asia Leather Fair (T/S/P)	World Trade Center Istanbul, Turkey January
China International Clothing and Accessories Fair (P)	Beijing, China April
Comispel International (P)	World Fashion Center Lausanne, Switzerland March

KEY: P = Products T = Tanners S = Suppliers

CALENDAR OF INTERNATIONAL FABRIC SHOWS

Name of Event	Details
Moda-In	Milan, Italy September (Fall) and March (Spring)
Prato Expo	Florence, Italy September (Fall) and March (Spring)

Name of Event	Details
Premier Vision	Paris, France October (Fall) and March (Spring)
Ideacomo	Lake Como, Italy October (Fall) and March (Spring)
International Fashion Fabric Exhibition	New York, NY October (Fall) and March (Spring)
Texitalia	New York, NY November (Fall) and April (Spring)
Interstoff	Frankfurt, Germany November (Fall) and April (Spring)

Publications

In the United States, it is often best to order foreign-published fashion magazines through a reputable magazine distributor than to attempt to subscribe to them directly. The magazines are quite expensive and often get "lost" in the mail.

KEY LEATHER PUBLICATIONS

Publication	Address	Frequency
Arpel	Italy	Four times per year
(Order through one of the magazine sources in Appendix C.)		
Outerwear Magazine	Fur Publishing Plus, Inc. 19 W. 21st St. New York, NY 10010	Monthly
Vogue Pelle	Italy	Six times per year
(Order through one of the magazine sources in Appendix C.)		

Publication	Address	Frequency
Colori in Pelle	Italy	Yearly
(Order through one of the magazine sources in Appendix C.)		
Le Cuir	14 Rue de la Folie-Regnaut 75011, Paris, France	Weekly
IDC Industrie Du Cuir	14 Rue de la Foile-Regnaut 75011, Paris, France	Monthly

OTHER IMPORTANT PUBLICATIONS

Publication	Address	Frequency
Women's Wear Daily (WWD)	7 West 34th St. New York, NY 10001-8191 800-289-0273	Daily
Daily News Record (DNR)	7 West 34th St. New York, NY 10001-8191 609-461-6248	Daily
Fashion Reporter	300 Park Ave South New York, NY 10010 212-477-2343	Bimonthly

FABRIC RESOURCE GUIDES

Trends in Progress (TIP)
P.O. Box 5161
New York, NY 10185
212-289-0267

Fashiondex
157 West 27th Street
New York, NY 10001
212-647-0051

FABRIC NEWSLETTERS

Sourcing News (U.S.)
Just Prints (U.S.)
P.O. Box 5161
New York, NY 10185
212-289-0267

Schools

Fashion Institute of Technology
Seventh Avenue at 27th Street
New York, NY 10001-5992
Telephone: 212-760-7667

What the school offers: Certificate program in either men's or women's leather apparel design

Lehr-Pruf-und Forschungsinstitut fur die Lederwirtschaft
Postfach 2944, D 7410,
Reutlingen, Germany
Telephone: 07121 4 0056
Fax: 07121 4 54 93

What the school offers: Training, research, and experimental institute for leather

National Institute of Fashion Technology (NIFT)
Hauz Khaus, Near Gulmohar Park
New Delhi, India 110016
Telephone: 3315038
Fax: 00-91-11-3322183

What the school offers: Two-year post-graduate diploma in leather garment design and technology

The National Leathersellers Centre
Nene College
Moulton Park, Northhampton NN2 7AL
England
Telephone: 0604 715000
Fax: 0604 720636

What the school offers: Study in the science of leather technology
and tanning

Resource Directory

CLEANING AND CARE PRODUCTS

Apple Brand® Products
Apple Polishes Inc.
P.O. Box 43
Stow, MA 01775
508-897-6569
800-322-6569
Fax: 508-897-9706
Products: Protectorants, leather cleaners
and conditioners, suede cleaners

Bick 4®
Bickmore Inc.
P.O. Box 279
Hudson, MA 01749
617-562-9172
Products: Leather conditioners, cleaners,
protectorants

Finis®
Vespro, Inc.
44 Montgomery, Suite 2874
San Francisco, CA 94104
415-434-3072
Fax: 415-459-7311
Products: Protectorants

Leather Lotion
Cadillac Leather Care
29200 Southfield Rd., Suite 208
Southfield, MI 48076
313-559-8200
Fax: 313-559-8652
Products: Leather cleaners/conditioners

Lexol®
Summit Industries, Inc.
P.O. Box 1214
Atlanta, GA 30301
404-524-5434
800-241-6996
Fax: 404-584-5172
Products: Leather cleaners/conditioners

Orkin of London®
Gem Touch, Inc.
1 Massey Square, 304
Toronto, Ontario, Canada M4C 5L4
416-699-5895
Fax: 416-759-8298
Products: Leather/suede protectorants,
cleaners, conditioners

PeleJez Leather, Inc.
5415 Casgrain Ave.
Montreal, Quebec, Canada H2T 1X4
514-279-4547
Fax: 514-279-6979
Products: Leather/suede protectorants,
cleaners, conditioners

Pollack's
222 West 29th St.
New York, NY 10001
212-564-8051
800-422-7467
Fax: 212-268-9593
Products: Leather cleaners, dyes

Tana Style 16®
Kiwi Brands, Inc.
Route 662
Douglasville, PA 19518
800-523-1210
Fax: 215-385-6177

Pierre Square
8505 Dalton Rd.
Montreal, Quebec, Canada H4T FV5
514-341-5350
Fax: 514-737-1650
Products: Leather/suede protectorants,
leather/suede cleaners, conditioners

The Leather Solution
Total Leather Care
3500 B Hampton Rd.
Oceanside, NY 11572
516-536-8383
Fax: 516-536-8442
Product: Leather cleaners, conditioners,
protectorants

Vectra Apparel Supply
Vectra Enterprises, Inc.
351 Peachtree Hills Ave., Suite 224
Atlanta, GA 30305
800-241-4982
Fax: 404-266-3493
Products: Leather/suede protectorants

CLEANERS

Arrow Leathercare Services
3838 Troost Ave.
Kansas City, MO 64109
816-931-2452
800-54-ARROW
Fax: 816-931-0300

Morrison Suede and Leather Works
401E 17th Ave., Unit C
Denver, CO 80203
303-894-9911

Leathercraft Process
1 St. George Ave.
Roselle, NJ 07203
201-241-2600

Premier Suede and Leather Cleaner
3098 N. California Street
Burbank, CA 91504
800-245-2378
818-842-2151

Ram Leather Care
2402 West Tusc. Street
Canton, OH 44708
216-454-2756

Ram Leather Care
11 Humphreys St.
Dorchester, MA 02125
617-265-8162

968 Klondike Port
Conyers, GA 30207
404-483-3454

The Suede Shop
506 30th Street
Vienna, WV 26105

Leather-Rich Inc.
210 Silver Lake Rd.
Oconomowac, WI 53066
800-365-0230
In Wisconsin: 800-242-9552

Leathercare Inc.
901 Elliot W
Seattle, WA 98119
206-285-2225

Brownie's Suede and Leather
6571 Westminster Blvd.
Westminster, CA 92683
714-893-0085

Wholesale Protectorants and Cleaners
AceGuard by Ace Fur Blending
208 W. 29th St.
New York, NY 10001
212-947-5931

Kirk's Suede Life, Inc.
2501 West Fulton Street
Chicago, IL 60612
312-733-6611
800-444-KIRK
Fax: 312-666-8530

Scotchgard® by 3M
3M Center Bldg. 301-1E-03
St. Paul, MN 55144
612-736-1587

RETAIL LEATHER SUPPLIERS

Libra Leather
Contact: Mitchel Alfus
259 West 30th St.
New York, NY 10001
212-695-3114

Strong & Fisher
Contact: Ann Sampson
470 Seventh Ave.
New York, NY 10018
212-465-1503

Leatherfacts
Contact: Francois George
262 West 38th St.
New York, NY 10018
212-382-2788

Leather Suede Skins
Contact: Faina Golub
261 West 35th St.
New York, NY 10018
212-967-6616

Global Leather Co.
Contact: Paul Crystal
214 West 29th St.
New York, NY 10001
212-244-5190
Fax: 212-594-7515

Alliance Leather
Contact: Martin Gross
352 Seventh Avenue
New York, NY 10001
212-736-7044
Fax: 212-736-7045

R & G Leather
Contact: Dave Glass
46-55 Metropolitan Ave.
Ridgewood, NY 11385
212-565-0340

MAGAZINE SOURCES

Design Inspiration
488 Seventh Ave.
New York, NY 10018
212-736-1537

Mady Jenny
1501 Broadway
New York, NY 10036
212-944-8460

Yarn Collar Library
1369 Broadway
New York, NY 10018
212-279-0611

Margit Publications
1412 Broadway
New York, NY 10018
212-302-5137

LEATHER GARMENT MANUFACTURING SUPPLIES

Active Trimming
250 West 39th St.
New York, NY 10018
212-921-7114
Products: Glover's needles, cold tape, awls, cutting blades, cement and thinner, cutting table dressing oil, double-faced tape, granite tag boards, fusible webbing, glazed thread

Master Cutting Room
50 West 27th St.
New York, NY 10001
212-889-8188
Products: Leather cutting table tops, cutting blades and tools, table dressing oil

A & B Leather Findings
500 W. 57th St.
New York, NY 10019
212-265-8124
Products: Leather glues

Fox Sewing Machine
307 West 38th St.
New York, NY 10018
212-594-2438
Products: Leather sewing machine teflon teeth, plate, foot, needles

Myron Zuckerman
111 West 25th St.
New York, NY 10001
212-255-6929
Products: Leather sewing machines, teflon teeth, plate, foot, needles

SUPPORT MATERIALS

Dupont Performance Insulation
P.O. Box 80705
Wilmington, DE 19805
800-342-7345
Product: Insulation products

3M
3M Center Building 275-6W-01
St. Paul, MN 55144-1000
Product: Insulation products

FASHION COLOR/TREND FORECAST SERVICES

Here & There Inc.
10 West 40th Street
New York, NY 10018
212-354-9014

Promostyl
80 West 40th Street
New York, NY 10018
212-921-7930

Pat Tunsky
1040 Avenue of the Americas
New York, NY 10018
212-944-9160

Trend Union
90 Riverside Drive
New York, NY 10024
212-724-3825

Norma Morris Design Products
1412 Broadway
New York, NY 10018
212-724-0758

Fashion Dossier
1559 Broadway
New York, NY 10018
212-967-1919

Doneger 3
463 7th Ave.
New York, NY 10018
212-967-1605

Color Box
29 West 38th St.
New York, NY 10018
212-921-1399

Color Perspective
488 7th Ave.
New York, NY 10018
212-563-4604

Bureau De Styl
989 Avenue of the Americas
New York, NY 10018
212-947-4600

The Fashion Service
1412 Broadway
New York, NY 10018
212-704-0035

Ellen Sideri (ESP)
12 West 37th St.
New York, NY 10018
212-629-9200

FIBER COMPANIES FOR COLOR/TREND INFORMATION

Cotton Inc.
1370 Avenue of the Americas
New York, NY 10019
212-586-1070

E. I. Dupont of Nemours
1251 Avenue of the Americas
New York, NY 10020
212-512-9200

Hoechst Celanese
2 Park Ave.
New York, NY 10016
212-251-8000

The Wool Bureau
360 Lexington Avenue
New York, NY 10017
212-986-6222

COLOR SERVICES

The Color Association of the United States
109 West 44th St.
New York, NY 10036
212-582-6884

Dixie Yarns
1071 Avenue of the Americas
New York, NY 10018
212-869-1181

Huepoint
39 West 37th St.
New York, NY 10018
212-921-2025

Pantone
590 Commerce Blvd.
Carlstadt, NJ 07072
201-935-5500

Glossary

abattoir: slaughterhouse

aniline: very soft skins without any sprayed-on additives

basifying agents: chemical agents used to neutralize acidity

bating: the process of using vinegar to neutralize the lime in an animal's skin

bleeding (or staining): refers to the migration of dye in a solution from the leather into another material, caused by perspiration, laundering, or wet weather exposure, largely controlled by the tanner's choice of dye and dyeing conditions

blocking: the adhesion of a leather finish to itself

braccae: leather trousers

bundle: a twelve-unit skin

chrome: the key element in chromium sulfate, which transforms the natural proteins in skins to inert substances that resist rotting

cockles: bruise marks; veins which appear in irregular patterns on raw skin

cold tape: a woven tape with a glove at one side used to control stretch in certain areas of a garment

crocking: the physical transfer of color through a rubbing action

crust: a dried, raw animal skin

curing: a process that protects animal skins from rotting

cuts (or cut lines): the seams required to make a garment

double hiding: a condition where the grain layer is actually separated from the inner corium layer of an animal skin

English domestic: lambskin that comes from England

fat liquor: a mandatory additive used in the tanning process, as it adds oils to animal skins and returns the skins to their natural softness

fitting muslin: a first sample of muslin for the purpose of testing the garment for proper fit

flaying: removing skin from an animal carcass, by hand and/or machine

fusible interfacing: a support material sold by the yard, which has a gummed adhesive back used to add stiffness to certain areas of a garment

grain side: inside and outside of an animal skin

hand: the overall feel of a skin, i.e., its stiffness versus its softness

hide: the pelt on a large animal

marking and scissor method: an alternative to the short knife method, in which a waterproof marking pen is used to trace around a pattern piece with a pencil or fine tipped waterproof marking pen to mark all notches; sharp dressmaking shears, usually seven inches or ten inches in length, are used to cut pattern pieces

mood boards: theme or concept boards that help the designer sell a particular line to a target customer

nappa: the outside, formerly fur-bearing side of an animal skin, worn on the outside of a garment

neutralization: a wet process used in tanning, where wet blues are processed with specific ingredients designed to make animal skins lighter, softer, harder, and so on

oak tag patterns: a pattern made for oak tag paper

oil tanning: leather tanned with animal oils and/or fish oils, produces very soft leather

over-splitting: splitting a thick hide into pieces of leather that are too thin

pack: represents approximately 3,000 square feet of leather

pickle: treating animal skins with a mixture of water, salt, and sulfuric acid for approximately two hours

pipey grain: a loose, coarse, puckered appearance on the grain surface of an animal skin

puering: a process where animal hides are treated with natural enzymes found in animal excrement, employed before the era of modern tanning

semi-aniline: any skin that undergoes a surface treatment, which involves spraying animal skins with coats of dye or plastic film, which is designed to obscure flaws

setting out: the wringing-out of animal skins, part of the skin-storing process

setting out machine: a large machine with two rollers which wring out excess moisture in animal skins, part of the skin-storing process

shading: caused by uneven dyeing, this condition exists when different parts of a skin show variations in color

short knife: a small knife with replaceable blades that is sharpened on a special stone and used to cut animal skins

side leather: skins usually from the horse, cow, and buffalo that are cut in half by tanners before being shipped to manufacturers (also called "half hides")

skin: the pelt of a small animal

spew (or fatty spew): a leather that develops a white hazy deposit on its surface

splits: cow skin that can be split into two skins, due to the fact that it is a thicker skin

staking process: stretching animal skins to their normal sizes without rewetting them

suede: the inside of an animal skin, worn on the outside of a garment; leather with a napped surface

tackiness: a condition where leather feels tacky or sticky and will adhere to almost anything it touches; the condition is usually due to inadequate drying or curing of the finish system

tan: to convert (a hide) into leather

tannery: a factory that buys raw skins, makes the skins into leather, colors the leather, and sells it to garment manufacturers

tannin: a substance of plant origin that has a tanning effect, used in tanning and dyeing

weight: the number of ounces per square foot of skin

wet blues: defleshed, pickled animal skins which have added to them chromium sulfate powder, among other ingredients, which are rotated in drums for roughly eight hours; skins turn a light-colored blue when they emerge from the drums

white handkerchief test: a test used to confirm the stability of a garment's color by rubbing a handkerchief along the inner facing of the garment; the color should not easily come off

Bibliography

Churchill, James. 1983. *The Complete Book of Tanning Skins and Furs.* Harrisburg, PA: Stackpole Books.

Delano, Joseph. 1974. *The New Book of Leatherwork: Projects for Today.* Drake Publishers.

DiValentin, Maria M. 1972. *Getting Started in Leathercraft.* New York: Collier Books.

Furst, Ronald Kenneth. 1974. *Soft Suede, Supple Leather.* New York: Simon and Schuster.

Gustavson, K. H. 1956. *The Chemistry of Tanning Processes.* New York: Academic Press.

Hamilton-Head, Ian. 1979. *Leatherwork.* Poole Dorset: Blandford Press.

James, Laurie. 1990. Cleaning and Care: Build Sales and Repeat Business. *Leather Today,* December.

Leather Industries of America. 1975. *Leather in Our Lives.* Rev. ed. Washington, D.C.

Leather Industries of America and the United States Hide, Skin, and Leather Association. 1985. *Trade Practices for Proper Packer Cattlehide Delivery.* Arlington, VA: Leather Industries of America and the United States Hide, Skin, and Leather Association. Washington, D.C.

Leathercraft Process. (1984). *Purchasing Suede and Leather Garments.* New York: Leathercraft Process.

Loeb, Jo. 1975. T*he Leather Book: Leather Clothes & Furniture You Can Make Yourself.* Englewood Cliffs, NJ: Prentice Hall, Inc.

Manning, Mary, and E. A. Manning. 1974. *Leatherwork: A Step-by-Step Guide.* London: Hamlyn Publishing Group.

Minnoch, John, and Sterling Robert Minnoch. 1979. *Hides and Skins.* Sioux City, IA: National Hide Association.

Morris, Ben, and Elizabeth Morris. 1975. *Making Clothes in Leather.* Englewood Cliffs, NJ: Taplinger Publishing Company.

Moseley, G. C. 1986. *Leather Goods Manufacture: Methods and Processes.* West Orange, N.J.: A. Saifer.

O'Flaherty, Fred, William T. Roddy, and Robert M. Lollar, eds. [1956-65] 1978. Reprint. *The Chemistry and Technology of Leather.* 4 vols. Huntington, N.Y.: R. E. Krieger Publishing Company.

Parker, Xenia Ley. 1972. *Working with Leather.* New York: Charles Scribner's Sons.

Sharphouse, J. H. 1983. *Leather Technician's Handbook.* Moulton Park: Leather Producer's Association.

Thorstensen, Thomas C. [1969] 1976. Reprint. *Practical Leather Technology.* 2d rev. ed. Malabar, FL: R. E. Krieger Publishing Company.

Waterer, John W. 1946. *Leather in Life, Art, and Industry.* London: Faber and Faber

Welsh, Peter C. 1964. A Craft that Resisted Change: American Training Practices to 1850. *Technology and Culture,* 1963. Dearborn Michigan: Technology and Culture.

Index